GREAT COOKING MADE EASY

SLIMMERS' DELIGHTS

Better Homes and Gardens
TRADEMARK

TREASURE PRESS

BETTER HOMES AND GARDENS BOOKS

Editor Gerald M. Knox
Art Director Ernest Shelton
Managing Editor David A. Kirchner
Project Editors James D. Blume, Marsha Jahns
Project Managers Liz Anderson, Jennifer Speer Ramundt, Angela K. Renkoski

Diet Recipes (American edition)
Editor Maureen Powers
Project Manager Marsha Jahns
Graphic Designer Tom Wegner
Electronic Text Processor Donna Russell
Photographers Michael Jensen, Sean Fitzgerald
Food Stylists Marilyn Cornelius, Janet Herwig, Maria Rolandelli

Slimmers' Delights (British edition)
Project Managers Liz Anderson, Angela K. Renkoski
Assistant Art Director Tom Wegner
Contributing Project Editors Irena Chalmers Books, Inc., and associates: Jean Atcheson, Irena Chalmers, Ann Chase, Mary Dauman, Cathy Garvey, Mary Goodbody, Terri Griffing, Margaret Homberg, Kathryn Knapp, Stephanie Lyness, Susan Anderson Nabel, Victoria Proctor, Elizabeth Wheeler
Electronic Text Processors Alice Bauman, Kathy Benz, Paula Forest, Vicki Howell, Mary Mathews, Joyce Wasson

This edition first published in Great Britain in 1989 by:

Treasure Press
Michelin House
81 Fulham Road
London, SW3 6RB

Original edition published by Meredith Corporation in the United States of America.

BETTER HOMES AND GARDENS is a registered trademark in Canada, New Zealand, South Africa, and other countries.

ISBN 1 85051 435 6

Produced by Mandarin Offset
Printed and bound in Hong Kong

"**I**'m on a diet" is a familiar refrain. Whether you're a serious dieter or a casual calorie counter, it's important to get the most from the calories you consume. That's why you need dishes that not only fill you up and provide needed nutrients, but also taste terrific! Because main dishes provide the majority of the calories in a meal—and most of your daily protein requirements—they're the most important dishes in *any* diet.

The recipes in this book were chosen with those needs in mind. You'll find them long on variety and flavour, but short on calories. A calorie count, based on the American ingredients, is listed with each recipe.

Take a look at *Slimmers' Delights*. Turn the page and start creating hearty soups, garden-fresh salads, delicate pancakes, mouth-watering quiches, and much, much more. Dieting has never been so delicious!

Contents

Tempting Casseroles

Look no further for slimming, quick-to-fix casseroles. Our recipes prove that hearty, one-dish meals don't need to be high in calories or time-consuming to prepare. Try one for supper tonight. In just minutes you'll have tantalizing results.

Salmon-Rice Bake

Salmon-Rice Bake

10	ounces (275g) frozen peas
16	ounces (450g) tinned salmon, drained
7½	ounces (210g) tinned semi-condensed cream of mushroom soup
8	fluid ounces (220ml) skimmed milk
4	ounces (110g) grated cheddar cheese
5	ounces (150g) quick-cooking rice
2	teaspoons minced dried onion
¼	teaspoon dried dill

307 calories per serving

In a colander run hot water over peas for about 1 minute or until thawed (see photo 1). Drain peas well. Remove skin and bones from salmon (see photo 2). Break salmon into large chunks. In a medium casserole mix peas, soup, milk, cheese, uncooked rice, onion, and dill. Gently stir in salmon. Cover casserole (see photo 3). Bake in a 350°F (180°C) gas mark 4 oven for 50 minutes. Remove the casserole from the oven. Let stand, covered, for 10 minutes. Makes 6 servings.

1 To quickly thaw frozen vegetables, place them in a colander and rinse under hot tap water for about 1 minute.

2 Using your fingers, pull apart the sections of tinned salmon, then remove the bones and skin, being careful to keep the fish in chunks. The chunks will make the finished dish more attractive.

3 Cover the casserole to keep food moist during baking. If your dish doesn't have a lid, use a piece of foil slightly larger than the top of the dish. Shape the foil over the dish, sealing the edges.

Turkey-Vegetable Casserole

The whole family will enjoy this homely casserole, never suspecting it's a diet recipe.

10	ounces (275g) frozen mixed vegetables
6	ounces (175g) sliced turkey
10¾	ounces (290g) tinned condensed cream of chicken soup
8	fluid ounces (220ml) hot water
3	ounces (75g) quick-cooking barley
1	teaspoon poultry seasoning
¼	teaspoon onion powder

247 calories per serving

In a colander run hot water over vegetables for about 1 minute or until thawed (see photo 1). Drain vegetables well. Place turkey in a stack, then cut it all at once into thin strips

In a medium casserole dish combine soup, water, barley, poultry seasoning, and onion powder. Stir in thawed vegetables and turkey. Cover the casserole (see photo 3). Bake in a 350°F (180°C) gas mark 4 oven for 65 minutes, stirring once. Remove the casserole from the oven. Let stand, covered, for 10 minutes. Makes 6 servings.

Scrumptious Sandwiches

Ordinary sandwiches become extraordinary simply by changing the bread you use! Pick a pitta pocket, a flour tortilla, or sliced whole wheat bread. Then, turn the page for an impressive display of scrumptious fillings.

Tangy Beef and Swiss Sandwiches

Tangy Beef and Swiss Sandwiches

- **4 ounces (110g) natural low-fat yogurt**
- **1 tablespoon snipped parsley**
- **1 tablespoon finely grated carrot**
- **¼ teaspoon garlic salt *or* onion salt**
- **⅛ teaspoon dried basil *or* tarragon, crushed**
- **4 ounces (110g) thinly sliced cooked beef**
- **4 ounces (110g) Swiss cheese**
- **2 ounces (50g) chopped cucumber**
- **3 ounces (75g) coarsely chopped tomato**
- **2 ounces (50g) chopped green pepper**
- **4 leaves leaf lettuce**
- **2 ounces (50g) alfalfa sprouts**
- **4 slices whole wheat bread, 2 large pitta bread rounds, *or* four 8-inch (20cm) flour tortillas**

190 calories per serving for filling

In a small bowl combine yogurt, parsley, carrot, garlic or onion salt, and basil or tarragon. Mix well, then cover and chill.

Cut beef and cheese into thin, matchlike strips (julienne strips). In a bowl mix beef, cheese, cucumber, tomato, and green pepper. Add yogurt mixture (see photo 1). Toss gently to coat. Prepare sandwiches using lettuce; sprouts; and bread (see photo 2), pitta bread (see photo 3), or tortillas (see photo 4). Serves 4.

1 Add the yogurt mixture to the beef and Swiss cheese mixture all at once. Gently toss the ingredients together until all of the beef and cheese mixture is coated. This careful stirring keeps the cheese from breaking into pieces.

2 Make open sandwiches by using four slices of whole wheat bread. Line each slice of bread with a lettuce leaf, then spoon the beef and Swiss cheese mixture onto the bread. Cut each sandwich in half diagonally with a sharp knife, as shown. Top each sandwich with some of the alfalfa sprouts. (258 calories per serving)

3 Create pitta pocket sandwiches by cutting two large pitta bread rounds in half crosswise with a sharp kitchen knife. If necessary, gently slip a knife into each pitta pocket to loosen the sides so the pocket will open easily without tearing. Line each pocket with a lettuce leaf. Spoon the beef and Swiss cheese mixture into the pockets, as shown. Top each pitta sandwich with some of the alfalfa sprouts. (230 calories per serving)

4 Assemble open tortilla sandwiches by using four 8-inch (20cm) tortillas. Buy ready-to-use flour tortillas in the refrigerated section of the supermarket or delicatessen. Top each flour tortilla with a lettuce leaf. Spoon the beef and Swiss cheese mixture onto the tortillas. Top each tortilla with some of the alfalfa sprouts, as shown. (285 calories per serving)

Egg Salad Surprise

6 hard-cooked eggs, chopped
1 medium tomato, seeded and chopped
3 ounces (75g) sliced celery
2 ounces (50g) cubed tangy cheddar
   cheese
4 ounces (110g) tinned chopped green
   chilli peppers, drained
2 ounces (50g) soured cream
1 tablespoon skimmed milk
¼ teaspoon salt
   Several dashes bottled hot pepper
   sauce
   Dash pepper
4 slices rye bread *or* wheat bread
4 leaves leaf lettuce

293 calories per serving

In a medium bowl combine eggs, tomato, celery, and cheese. For dressing, in a small bowl combine chilli peppers, soured cream, milk, salt, pepper sauce, and pepper. Pour dressing over egg mixture, then toss gently to coat (see photo 1, page 12). Chill 2 to 3 hours. To make open sandwiches, line each bread slice with a lettuce leaf. Spoon egg mixture onto bread slices, then cut each sandwich diagonally with a knife (see photo 2, page 12). Serves 4.

To make pitta sandwiches: Use two large *pitta bread rounds*. Cut bread in half crosswise. Line each pitta pocket with a lettuce leaf. Spoon egg mixture into pockets (see photo 3, page 13). Makes 4 servings. (265 calories per serving)

Cheese and Veggie Sandwiches

12 ounces (350g) low-fat cottage cheese,
   drained
1 ounce (25g) grated carrot
2 ounces (50g) chopped green pepper,
   radish, *or* celery
½ teaspoon finely snipped chives
2 ounces (50g) soured cream
4 slices whole wheat *or* white bread
2 tablespoons horseradish mustard
   Spinach leaves
4 slices tomato

188 calories per serving

In a medium bowl combine drained cheese; carrot; green pepper, radish, or celery; and chives. Add soured cream to cheese mixture (see photo 1, page 12). Stir to combine. To make open sandwiches, spread bread slices with horseradish mustard, then top with spinach leaves. Spoon cheese mixture onto bread slices. Top with a tomato slice. Cut each sandwich in half diagonally (see photo 2, page 12). Serves 4.

To make tortilla sandwiches: Use four 8-inch (20cm) *flour tortillas*. Spread tortillas with horseradish mustard, then top with spinach leaves. Spoon cheese mixture onto tortillas. Top with a tomato slice. Makes 4 servings. (215 calories per serving)

Curried Turkeywiches

Curry gets its golden colour from turmeric, one of 20 herbs and spices used in this seasoning blend

10	ounces (275g) diced cooked turkey *or* chicken
1	medium apple, cored and chopped
1	ounce (25g) chopped green pepper
3	ounces (75g) Neufchâtel cheese, softened
½	teaspoon curry powder
2	tablespoons orange juice
4	large pitta bread rounds
	Leaf lettuce

261 calories per serving

In a medium bowl combine turkey or chicken, apple, and green pepper. To make dressing, in a small bowl combine cheese and curry powder, then stir in orange juice until mixture is smooth. Add dressing to turkey mixture, then toss gently to coat (see photo 1, page 12). Chill several hours. If necessary, stir in additional orange juice to make desired consistency. To make pitta pockets, cut pitta bread in half crosswise. Line each pocket with lettuce. Spoon turkey mixture into pockets (see photo 3, page 13). Serves 4.

To make tortilla sandwiches: Use four 8-inch (20cm) *flour tortillas*. Top each tortilla with lettuce. Spoon turkey mixture onto tortillas. Makes 4 servings. (276 calories per serving)

Seaside Sandwiches

Using a tin of tuna in brine in place of the crab slashes the cost without sacrificing flavour.

6	ounces (175g) frozen crabmeat
2	hard-cooked eggs, chopped
1	ounce (25g) chopped fresh spinach, endive, *or* romaine
4	ounces (110g) chopped water chestnuts
1	tomato, peeled, seeded, and chopped
½	small cucumber, peeled, seeded, and chopped
2½	ounces (60g) soured cream
¼	teaspoon salt
¼	teaspoon finely grated lemon peel
4	8-inch (20cm) flour tortillas

232 calories per serving

Thaw crabmeat. Flake crabmeat, then drain well in a strainer. Press crabmeat with the back of a spoon against the sides of the strainer to remove excess liquid. In a medium bowl combine crabmeat; eggs; spinach, endive, or romaine; water chestnuts; tomato; and cucumber. In a small bowl combine soured cream, salt, and lemon peel, then gently stir it into crab mixture (see photo 1, page 12). To make tortilla sandwiches, spoon crab mixture onto tortillas. Makes 4 servings.

To make open, wheat sandwiches: Use four slices *whole wheat bread*. Spoon crab mixture onto bread slices. Cut each sandwich diagonally with a knife (see photo 2, page 12). Makes 4 servings. (204 calories per serving)

Refreshing Salads

Salads are a natural choice for dieters and anyone else looking for a light meal. Enhance your next salad with a homemade diet dressing that starts with our rich, creamy Salad Dressing Base. This tasty dressing base has less than *one-sixth* of the calories found in regular bottled mayonnaise!

Fruity Chicken Salad

Salad Dressing Base

1   tablespoon plain flour
2   teaspoons caster sugar
1   teaspoon mustard powder
6   fluid ounces (165ml) skimmed milk
2   slightly beaten egg yolks
3   tablespoons vinegar

15 calories per tablespoon

In a medium saucepan combine flour, sugar, mustard, and ½ teaspoon *salt*. Stir in milk gradually (see photo 1). Cook and stir until thickened and bubbly, then cook and stir 2 minutes more (see photo 2). Gradually stir some of the hot mixture into egg yolks (see photo 3). Return all to mixture in the saucepan. Return to a gentle boil, stirring constantly. Cook and stir 2 minutes more. Stir in vinegar. Place in screw-top jar. Cover; chill. Store in refrigerator for up to 1 week. Use in salad dressings or as sandwich spread. Makes 8 fluid ounces (220ml).

Fruity Chicken Salad

8   fluid ounces (220ml) Salad Dressing
     Base (see recipe, above)
1   teaspoon finely grated orange peel
2   tablespoons orange juice
1   small cantaloupe
6   ounces (175g) torn spinach
4   ounces (110g) torn Webb lettuce
1   pound (450g) diced cooked chicken
8   ounces (225g) strawberries, halved
4   ounces (110g) sliced celery

184 calories per serving

For dressing, prepare Salad Dressing Base. Stir in orange peel and juice. Cover and chill. Remove seeds from cantaloupe, then scoop out balls to make about 1 pound (450g) (see photo 4). In a large bowl mix melon, spinach, lettuce, chicken, strawberries, and celery. Spoon mixture into six salad bowls. Drizzle some dressing over each (see photo 5). Makes 6 servings.

1 Stir constantly as you gradually add the milk to the flour mixture. The milk and flour must be well combined to avoid lumps.

2 Cook mixture over medium-high heat till thickened and bubbly. Bubbles should break gently over the entire surface.

3 With a wire whisk or wooden spoon stir about 2 fluid ounces (55ml) of the hot mixture into the beaten egg yolks. Adding the egg yolks directly to the hot mixture would cook them too fast and cause curdling.

4 To make melon balls, scoop the fruit with a melon baller. Invert the melon baller and push it down into the fruit, rotating it to cut each ball.

5 Drizzle about 3 tablespoons of the orange-flavoured salad dressing evenly over the top of each salad just before serving.

Tempting Tuna Salad

To thaw the frozen loose-pack broccoli quickly, see photo 1, page 8.

5 **fluid ounces (140ml) Salad Dressing Base (see recipe, page 18)**
1½ **teaspoons French mustard**
¼ **teaspoon celery seed**
7 **ounces (200g) frozen chopped broccoli, thawed and drained**
2 **ounces (50g) grated cheddar cheese**
1 **ounce (25g) sliced stoned ripe olives**
1 **hard-cooked egg, chopped**
6½ **ounces (185g) tinned tuna in brine, drained and flaked**
  Leaf lettuce

213 calories per serving

For dressing, prepare Salad Dressing Base (see photos 1–3, page 18). In a bowl combine 5 fluid ounces (140ml) of the base, mustard, and celery seed, then cover and chill.

In a large bowl combine broccoli, cheese, olives, and egg. Pour dressing over broccoli mixture and toss to coat. Carefully stir in tuna, then cover and chill. Serve on lettuce-lined salad plates. Makes 4 servings.

Cheese and Fruit Salad

4 **fluid ounces (110ml) Salad Dressing Base (see recipe, page 18)**
1 **tablespoon honey**
½ **teaspoon poppy seed**
1 **pear, cored**
1 **apple, cored**
6 **ounces seedless black *or* green grapes, halved**
3 **ounces (75g) Swiss cheese, cubed**
3 **ounces (75g) cheddar cheese, cubed**
  Leaf lettuce

285 calories per serving

For dressing, prepare Salad Dressing Base (see photos 1–3, page 18). In a small bowl combine 4 fluid ounces (110ml) of the base, honey, and poppy seed, then mix well. Cover and chill.

Slice pear and apple into thin wedges. In a large bowl combine pear, apple, grapes, and cheeses. Pour dressing over fruit-cheese mixture, then toss to coat. Serve in a lettuce-lined salad bowl. Makes 4 servings.

Beef Eater's Bounty

Use left-over roast beef or buy ready-cooked roast beef for this hearty beef salad.

8 **fluid ounces (220ml) Salad Dressing Base (see recipe, page 18)**
2 **ounces (50g) crumbled blue cheese**
2 **ounces (50g) soured cream**
¼ **teaspoon coarsely ground pepper**
  Dash bottled hot pepper sauce
8 **ounces (225g) thinly sliced cooked beef**
1 **pound (450g) torn Webb lettuce**
4 **ounces (110g) fresh mushrooms, halved**
10 **cherry tomatoes, halved**
2 **thinly sliced spring onions**

203 calories per serving

For dressing, prepare Salad Dressing Base (see photos 1–3, page 18). In a small bowl combine base, *half* of the blue cheese, soured cream, pepper, and pepper sauce. Beat with a rotary whisk until almost smooth. Stir in remaining blue cheese, then cover and chill.

Cut beef into thin, matchlike strips (julienne strips). In a large bowl combine beef, lettuce, mushrooms, tomatoes, and onion. Spoon beef-vegetable mixture into individual salad bowls. Drizzle about 2 fluid ounces (55ml) of the dressing over each salad (see photo 5, page 19). Makes 6 servings.

Tropical Salmon Salad

To toast the coconut, place it in a shallow baking tin. Bake in a 350°F (180°C) gas mark 4 oven for 5 to 10 minutes or until lightly browned, stirring once or twice.

4   **fluid ounces (110ml) Salad Dressing Base (see recipe, page 18)**
8   **ounces (225g) tinned crushed pineapple (juice pack)**
⅛   **teaspoon ground ginger**
16   **ounces (450g) tinned salmon, drained**
4   **ounces (110g) chopped water chestnuts**
1   **ounce (25g) chopped green pepper Leaf lettuce**
1   **ounce (25g) desiccated coconut, toasted**

237 calories per serving

For dressing, prepare Salad Dressing Base (see photos 1–3, page 18). Drain pineapple, reserving 1 tablespoon juice. In a small bowl combine 4 fluid ounces (110ml) of the base, reserved pineapple juice, and ginger, then cover and chill.

Remove skin and bones from salmon (see photo 2, page 9). Flake salmon into a large bowl. Add drained pineapple, water chestnuts, and green pepper. Add dressing to salmon mixture and toss gently to coat. Cover and chill 2 hours.

Serve on four individual lettuce-lined salad plates. Sprinkle each salad with some of the toasted coconut. Makes 4 servings.

Summer Fruit-Chicken Salad

4   **fluid ounces (110ml) Salad Dressing Base (see recipe, page 18)**
2   **tablespoons honey**
1   **tablespoon vinegar**
1   **teaspoon lemon juice**
½   **teaspoon curry powder**
⅛   **teaspoon ground ginger**
1   **pound (450g) cubed cooked chicken**
4   **ounces (110g) thinly sliced celery**
1   **tablespoon thinly sliced spring onion**
3   **medium nectarines**
12   **ounces (350g) dark sweet cherries**
1   **ounce (25g) slivered almonds Leaf lettuce**

241 calories per serving

For dressing, prepare Salad Dressing Base (see photos 1–3, page 18). In a small bowl combine 4 fluid ounces (110ml) of the base, honey, vinegar, lemon juice, curry powder, and ginger. Cover and chill. In a large bowl mix chicken, celery, and onion, then cover and chill. Chill nectarines and cherries.

Spread almonds in a single layer in a shallow baking tin. Toast nuts in a 350°F (180°C) gas mark 4 oven for 10 to 12 minutes or until golden brown, stirring once.

Just before serving, stone and slice nectarines. Halve and stone cherries. Pour dressing over chicken mixture, then add nectarines, cherries, and almonds. Toss lightly to mix. Serve in a lettuce-lined bowl. Makes 6 servings.

Flavoursome Simmered Meats

Slow-cook less tender cuts of meat to mouth-watering perfection. Simply trim away separable fat, brown the meat without oil, and then simmer in a flavoursome liquid. Spicy Beef Stew is the perfect example of sensational eating. It's a rich beef stew, complemented by carrots, broccoli, and tomatoes. Indulge!

Spicy Beef Stew

Spicy Beef Stew

 1 **pound (450g) chuck *or* blade bone steak**
   Cooking oil
 4 **ounces (110g) chopped onion**
 1 **clove garlic, minced**
 1 **pound (450g) tinned tomatoes, cut up**
 ¾ **pint (425ml) water**
 ½ **pint (275ml) tinned condensed beef**
   broth
 1 **tablespoon chilli powder**
 ½ **teaspoon ground cumin**
 ½ **teaspoon dried basil, crushed**
 4 **large carrots**
10 **ounces (275g) frozen cut broccoli**
 2 **tablespoons cold water**
 1 **tablespoon cornflour**

160 calories per serving

Trim separable fat from meat (see photo 1). Cut meat into ¾-inch (2cm) cubes. Coat a large saucepan with cooking oil. Heat the saucepan. Cook meat, onion, and garlic in the saucepan over medium-high heat until meat is brown. Drain off fat. Stir in *undrained* tomatoes, water, broth, chilli powder, cumin, and basil. Bring mixture to boiling; reduce heat. Cover and simmer for 1½ hours or until meat is tender.

Cut carrots into thin matchlike sticks (julienne strips). Stir carrots and broccoli into stew mixture, then cover and simmer for 8 to 10 minutes more or until carrots and broccoli are crisp-tender (see photo 2).

In a small bowl combine cold water and cornflour (see photo 3). Stir into stew. Cook and stir until thickened and bubbly, then cook and stir for 2 minutes more. Makes 4 servings.

1 Trim away as much of the fat as possible from the meat to eliminate unnecessary calories. Use a sharp knife to cut off the separable fat—the fat that usually appears in a solid piece around the outside of the meat.

2 To test the vegetables for tenderness, insert a fork into several of them. Select the stalkier and tougher vegetables for testing. Carrots and the stalk of the broccoli, for example, will not cook as quickly as the floret portion of the broccoli.

When done, the vegetables should still be slightly crisp, but tender. This means that the fork will pierce the vegetables, but they will not feel mushy or fall apart.

3 Stir the cold water and cornflour together until the cornflour is dissolved. (If the mixture isn't used immediately, stir it again before using it, because the mixture will separate.) Slowly stir the cornflour mixture into the hot stew. This keeps the cornflour from lumping when added to the hot mixture.

Burgundy Beef

1 pound (450g) boneless chuck steak, cut
  ½ inch (1cm) thick
  Cooking oil
4 ounces (110g) coarsely grated carrot
4 ounces (110g) chopped onion
4 fluid ounces (110ml) burgundy
4 fluid ounces (110ml) water
1 clove garlic, minced
1 tablespoon cold water
1½ teaspoons cornflour

176 calories per serving

Trim separable fat from steak (see photo 1, page 24). Cut meat into four pieces. Pound with a meat mallet until the meat is about ¼ inch (½cm) thick (see photo 2, page 114). Sprinkle meat with salt and pepper. Coat a 10-inch (25.5cm) frying pan with cooking oil, then heat. Cook meat quickly in pan on both sides until meat is brown. Drain off fat.

Add carrot, onion, burgundy, 4 fluid ounces (110ml) water, and garlic to the frying pan. Bring mixture to boiling; reduce heat. Cover and simmer for 45 minutes or until meat is tender. Transfer meat to a serving dish and cover with foil to keep warm.

In a small bowl combine cold water and cornflour (see photo 3, page 25). Stir mixture into cooking liquid. Cook and stir until thickened and bubbly, then cook and stir 2 minutes more. Serve over meat. Makes 4 servings.

Veal Stew

12 ounces (350g) stewing veal
  Cooking oil
1 small onion, cut into thin wedges
16 ounces (450g) tinned stewed tomatoes,
  cut up
6 fluid ounces (165ml) tinned tomato
  juice
½ teaspoon dried thyme, crushed
3 medium carrots, sliced ½ inch (1cm)
  thick
1 medium turnip, peeled and coarsely
  chopped
1 tablespoon cornflour
1 tablespoon cold water

221 calories per serving

Trim separable fat from stewing meat (see photo 1, page 24). Cut meat into ¾-inch (2cm) cubes. Coat a large saucepan with cooking oil. Heat the saucepan. Cook meat and onion in the saucepan over medium-high heat until meat is brown. Drain off fat.

Add *undrained* tomatoes, tomato juice, and thyme to the saucepan. Bring mixture to boiling; reduce heat. Cover and simmer for 25 minutes. Stir in carrots and turnip. Cook for 25 to 30 minutes more or until meat and vegetables are tender (see photo 2, page 25).

In a small bowl combine cornflour and cold water (see photo 3, page 25). Add mixture to stew. Cook and stir until mixture is thickened and bubbly, then cook and stir 2 minutes more. Makes 4 servings.

Saucy Steaks

Arrange the juicy steaks over hot noodles, then smother them with the delicious beer-cheese sauce. You'll wish you were always on a diet!

12 ounces (350g) chuck *or* blade bone
    steak, cut ½ inch (1cm) thick
Cooking oil
10 ounces (275g) cheddar cheese sauce,
    made according to packet directions
6 fluid ounces (165ml) light beer
¾ teaspoon dried oregano, crushed
¼ teaspoon pepper
1 medium onion, sliced and separated
    into rings
3 ounces (75g) medium noodles

300 calories per serving

Trim separable fat from steak (see photo 1, page 24). Cut it into four serving-size pieces. Coat a 10-inch (25.5cm) frying pan with cooking oil and heat the frying pan. Cook meat in the frying pan on both sides until meat is brown. Drain off fat.

In a medium bowl combine sauce, beer, oregano, and pepper. Pour sauce mixture over steak, then top with onion. Cook, covered, for 1 hour or until meat is tender. Cook noodles according to package directions. Drain. Arrange noodles on a warm serving dish, and place steaks atop noodles. Pour sauce over steaks and noodles. Makes 4 servings.

Lamb Chops and Vegetables

Adding a small amount of dried mint gives this lamb dish a distinctive, yet delicate flavour. If you have fresh mint, use 1 tablespoon of snipped leaves.

4 lamb chops, cut ¾ inch (2cm) thick
    (1¼ pounds [560g])
Cooking oil
Salt
Pepper
2 fluid ounces (55ml) water
2 teaspoons instant chicken bouillon
    granules
1 teaspoon dried mint, crushed
6 ounces (175g) frozen small whole
    onions
1 medium green pepper, cut into strips
2 medium tomatoes, cut into wedges
Fresh mint sprigs (optional)

148 calories per serving

Trim separable fat from chops (see photo 1, page 24). Coat a 10-inch (25.5cm) frying pan with cooking oil. Heat the frying pan. Cook chops in the frying pan on both sides. Drain off fat. Season chops lightly with salt and pepper. Stir in water, bouillon granules, and mint. Bring mixture to boiling; reduce heat. Cover and simmer for 20 to 25 minutes or until chops are almost tender.

Add onions and green pepper to the pan. Simmer, covered, for 5 to 7 minutes more or until green pepper is crisp-tender. Add tomatoes and cook mixture, covered, for 3 minutes or until heated through. Garnish with mint sprigs, if desired. Makes 4 servings.

Tasty Stuffed Vegetables

Which of these delectably different stuffed vegetables should you try first? It's a tough decision. Whatever your choice, you'll find the result is the same—a whole meal tucked into one neat, edible packet.

Pork-and-Spinach-Filled Vegetables

Pork-and-Spinach-Filled Vegetables

Press the thawed spinach between several layers of kitchen paper to drain thoroughly.

5	**fluid ounces (140ml) water**
2	**ounces (50g) long grain rice**
2	**sliced spring onions**
1	**pound (450g) minced pork**
¼	**teaspoon garlic salt**
10	**ounces (275g) frozen chopped spinach, thawed and well drained**
7½	**ounces (210g) tinned semi-condensed cream of mushroom soup**
2	**tomatoes, peeled, seeded, and chopped**
½	**teaspoon ground sage**
⅛	**teaspoon pepper**
6	**green peppers, three 8-ounce (225g) courgettes (6 to 8 inches [15 to 20cm] long), *or* 6 large tomatoes**
3	**tablespoons grated Parmesan cheese**

278 calories per serving for filling

In a small saucepan combine water, rice, and spring onions. Bring mixture to boiling; reduce the heat to low. Cover with a tight-fitting lid and cook for 15 minutes. Don't lift the cover. Remove mixture from the heat and let it stand, covered, for 5 minutes.

Meanwhile, in a 10-inch (25.5cm) frying pan cook pork until it's brown. Drain off fat (see photo 1). Return meat to the pan and sprinkle with garlic salt. Add cooked rice, spinach, soup, chopped tomato, sage, and pepper to meat, then mix well.

Prepare vegetable shells using green peppers (see photo 2), courgettes (see photo 3), or tomatoes (see photo 4).

Sprinkle shells with salt, then place them in a 13x9x2-inch (32.5x23x5cm) baking dish. Spoon filling into shells (see photo 5). Bake shells in a 350°F (180°C) gas mark 4 oven for 25 minutes or until heated through. Top each with some of the cheese. Makes 6 servings.

1 To thoroughly drain the fat from the cooked minced meat, transfer the meat to a colander placed over a bowl. Let the meat stand a few minutes to drain, then discard the fat that's accumulated in the bowl.

2 Cut the stem ends from the green peppers; remove the seeds. (If necessary, cut a thin slice from the pepper bottoms so they will stand up.) Chop the pepper tops to make 2 ounces (50g), then stir it into the pork mixture. In a medium saucepan cook the peppers, covered, in a large amount of boiling water for 3 to 5 minutes. Remove the peppers and invert them on kitchen paper to drain. (294 calories per serving)

3 Cut courgettes in half lengthwise. Cut and scoop out the pulp, leaving a ¼-inch (½cm) edge, as shown. Chop 4 ounces (110g) pulp; stir it into the pork mixture. Place the shells, cut side down, in a 10-inch (25.5cm) frying pan with 4 fluid ounces (110ml) water. Cover and simmer for 4 minutes. Remove the shells. Invert them on kitchen paper to drain. (291 calories per serving)

5 Stuff vegetable shells by lightly spooning the filling into the shells. Be careful to divide the filling (and calories) evenly.

4 Cut a thin slice from the stem end of each tomato. Scoop out the centre with a spoon. Reserve the pulp for another use. Invert the tomatoes on kitchen paper to drain. (318 calories per serving)

Greek-Style Stuffed Tomatoes

Traditional Greek favourites are in this savoury filling.

1 **pound (450g) minced lamb**
4 **ounces (110g) chopped onion**
6 **ounces (175g) peeled and diced aubergine**
6 **fluid ounces (165ml) water**
2 **ounces (50g) bulgur wheat**
2 **ounces (50g) raisins**
1 **ounce (25g) snipped parsley**
1 **beaten egg**
4 **ounces (110g) natural low-fat yogurt**
¼ **teaspoon ground cinnamon**
¼ **teaspoon ground nutmeg**
6 **large tomatoes**
3 **ounces (75g) natural low-fat yogurt (optional)**

196 calories per serving

In a 10-inch (25.5cm) frying pan cook lamb and onion until meat is brown and onion is tender, then drain off fat (see photo 1, page 30). Add aubergine, water, bulgur wheat, raisins, and parsley. Bring mixture to boiling; reduce heat. Cover and simmer for 15 minutes, stirring occasionally. Remove from the heat.

In a small bowl combine egg, 4 ounces (110g) yogurt, cinnamon, and nutmeg, then mix well. Add to meat mixture and salt to taste.

Cut off stem end of tomatoes. Scoop out pulp (see photo 4, page 31). Invert shells on kitchen paper to drain. Reserve tops and pulp for another use. Sprinkle shells with salt, then place them in a 13x9x2-inch (32.5x23x5cm) baking dish. Spoon lamb mixture into shells (see photo 5, page 31). Bake, covered, in a 350°F (180°C) gas mark 4 oven for 20 to 25 minutes or until heated through. To serve, dollop each shell with some yogurt, if desired. Makes 6 servings.

Ham-and-Rice-Stuffed Green Peppers

5 **ounces (150g) quick-cooking rice**
8 **ounces (225g) diced fully cooked ham**
8 **ounces (220ml) tinned sieved tomatoes**
2½ **ounces (60g) tinned sliced mushrooms, drained**
1 **tablespoon snipped parsley**
1 **teaspoon Worcestershire sauce**
¼ **teaspoon chilli powder**
Dash bottled hot pepper sauce
4 **large green peppers**

205 calories per serving

Cook rice according to package directions. In a large bowl combine rice, ham, sieved tomatoes, mushrooms, parsley, Worcestershire sauce, chilli powder, and pepper sauce, then mix well.

Remove tops from green peppers; set tops aside. Remove membrane and seeds from peppers (see photo 2, page 31). Cook peppers and tops in boiling water for 3 to 5 minutes; remove and invert on kitchen paper to drain. Sprinkle shells with salt, then place them in an 8x8x2-inch (20x20x5cm) baking dish. Spoon ham mixture into shells (see photo 5, page 31). Place tops of peppers over mixture. Bake in a 350°F (180°C) gas mark 4 oven for 20 to 25 minutes or until heated through. Makes 4 servings.

Taco-Filled Courgette Shells

1	pound (450g) lean minced beef
4	ounces (110g) chopped onion
2	tablespoons chopped green pepper
1	clove garlic, minced
1	tomato, peeled, seeded, and chopped
2	tablespoons tomato puree
2	tablespoons water
1½	teaspoons chilli powder
¼	teaspoon salt
¼	teaspoon ground red pepper
3	eight-ounce courgettes, 6 to 8 inches (15 to 20cm) long
2	ounces (50g) grated cheddar cheese Shredded lettuce (optional)

190 calories per serving

In a 10-inch (25.5cm) frying pan cook beef, onion, green pepper, and garlic until beef is brown and vegetables are tender. Drain off fat (see photo 1, page 30). Stir in tomato, tomato puree, water, chilli powder, salt, and red pepper.

Halve each courgette lengthwise. Scoop out pulp, leaving a ¼-inch (½cm) shell (see photo 3, page 31). Chop enough pulp to make 8 ounces (225g), then stir into beef mixture Place shells, cut side down, in a frying pan. Add 4 fluid ounces (110ml) *water* and bring to boiling. Cover and simmer for 4 to 5 minutes or just until tender; remove and invert on kitchen paper to drain. Sprinkle shells with salt, then place them in a 13x9x2-inch (32.5x23x5cm) baking dish. Spoon beef mixture into shells (see photo 5, page 31). Spoon excess filling around shells.

Cover and bake in a 350°F (180°C) gas mark 4 oven for 25 to 30 minutes or until heated through. Sprinkle each shell with some of the cheese and lettuce, if desired. Makes 6 servings.

Turkey-Stuffed Tomato Shells

1	pound (450g) diced cooked turkey *or* chicken
7½	ounces (210g) tinned semi-condensed cream of mushroom soup
3	ounces (75g) chopped celery
2½	ounces (60g) tinned sliced mushrooms, drained
2	tablespoons chopped pimento
1	tablespoon snipped parsley
¼	teaspoon dried thyme, crushed
4	large tomatoes
1	ounce (25g) grated cheddar *or* Swiss cheese

219 calories per serving

In a medium bowl combine turkey or chicken, soup, celery, mushrooms, pimento, parsley, and thyme, then mix well.

Cut off stem ends of tomatoes. Scoop out pulp (see photo 4, page 31). Invert shells on kitchen paper to drain. Reserve tops and pulp for another use.

Sprinkle shells with salt, then place them in an 8x8x2-inch (20x20x5cm) baking dish. Spoon turkey mixture into shells (see photo 5, page 31). Spoon any excess filling around shells. Bake, uncovered, in a 350°F (180°C) gas mark 4 oven for 20 to 25 minutes or until heated through. Sprinkle each shell with some of the cheddar or Swiss cheese. Makes 4 servings.

Savoury Soups

It's hard to resist the aroma and flavour of a piping hot bowl of soup, especially if it's homemade.

Whether you opt for an exotic Oriental-style soup or a hearty seafood chowder, you'll find these satisfying soups are worth the effort of starting from scratch. They're packed with flavour and trimmed of every possible calorie.

Oriental Soup

Chicken Stock

Bony chicken pieces (backs, necks, and wings) from 2 chickens
2 **large stalks celery with leaves, cut up**
2 **carrots, cut up**
1 **large onion, cut up**
2 **sprigs parsley**
1 **bay leaf**
½ **teaspoon dried thyme, crushed**
2 **whole cloves**

2 calories per cup

In a large covered flameproof casserole place chicken, celery, carrots, onion, parsley, bay leaf, thyme, cloves, ½ teaspoon *salt*, and ¼ teaspoon *pepper*. Add 2 pints plus 8 fluid ounces (1 litre, 220ml) water. Bring to boiling; reduce heat. Cover and simmer for 1¼ hours. Remove chicken and strain stock (see photo 1). Discard chicken, vegetables, and seasonings. Clarify stock, if desired (see tip box, page 39).

If using the stock hot, skim off fat (see photo 2). *Or*, chill stock for 6 to 8 hours and lift off fat (see photo 3). Makes 2 pints plus 4 fluid ounces (1 litre, 110ml).

Oriental Soup

32 **fluid ounces (900ml) Chicken Stock (see recipe, left)**
6 **ounces (175g) fresh mange tout or 6 ounces frozen mange tout, thawed**
10 **ounces (275g) diced fully cooked ham**
3 **ounces (75g) sliced fresh mushrooms or 4 ounces (110g) tinned sliced mushrooms, drained**
2 **sliced spring onions**
2 **tablespoons rice wine vinegar (optional)**

171 calories per serving

Prepare Chicken Stock. Clean fresh mange tout and remove strings (see photo 4). Slice mange tout in half crosswise. Set aside. In a large saucepan combine Chicken Stock, ham, and mushrooms. Bring to boiling; reduce heat. Cover and simmer for 4 to 5 minutes.

Stir in mange tout and spring onion (see photo 5). Cook 2 to 3 minutes more or until mange tout are crisp-tender. Stir in vinegar, if desired. Ladle into soup bowls. Makes 4 servings.

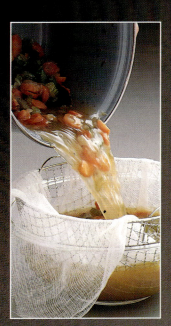

1 Use a double layer of cheesecloth to line a colander or large sieve. Place it over a large bowl. Strain the prepared stock by pouring it through the colander or sieve, as shown. Discard the bones, meat, vegetables, and seasonings caught by the cheesecloth.

2 If you want to use the stock right away, remove the fat while the stock is still hot. Use a metal spoon to skim off the oily liquid (fat) that rises to the top.

3 If time allows, make the stock ahead and chill it. When the fat solidifies, remove it by lifting it off with a spoon. Chilling the stock allows you to remove a larger amount of the fat more easily than you can when the stock is hot.

4 Remove the string from the mange tout by making a cut with a paring knife across the stem end of each pod and gently pulling down on the cut portion.

5 Mange tout are best when served crisp-tender. That's why they're added to the soup during the last few minutes of cooking.

Beef Stock (2 calories per cup): Prepare Chicken Stock (see recipe, page 36), *except* substitute 3 pounds (1kg350g) *meaty beef soup bones* (neck, leg, shank, or marrow bones) for chicken pieces. Place bones in a large shallow roasting tin. Bake, uncovered, in a 450°F (230°C) gas mark 8 oven for 30 minutes or until bones are well browned, turning occasionally. Drain off fat. Place browned bones in a covered casserole. Continue recipe as directed.

Chicken-Barley Soup

2 **pints (1 litre, 140ml) Chicken Stock (see recipe, page 36)**
1 **ounce (25g) quick-cooking barley**
1 **bay leaf**
1 **teaspoon dried basil, crushed**
¾ **teaspoon salt**
½ **teaspoon dried savory, crushed**
6 **ounces (175g) loose-pack frozen cut French beans, *or* peas**
4 **ounces (110g) thinly sliced carrots**
10 **ounces (275g) cooked chicken, cut into ½-inch (1cm) cubes**

126 calories per serving

Prepare Chicken Stock (see photos 1–3, page 36). In a large saucepan combine Chicken Stock, barley, bay leaf, basil, salt, and savory. Add vegetables and bring to boiling; reduce heat. Cover and simmer for 12 to 15 minutes or until barley and vegetables are tender. Remove bay leaf. Add chicken, then heat through. Ladle into soup bowls. Makes 6 servings.

Shellfish Soup

1¼ **pints (720ml) Chicken Stock (see recipe, page 36)**
3 **medium carrots, cut into julienne strips**
5 **ounces (150g) sliced celery**
6 **ounces (175g) frozen sweet corn**
2 **tablespoons snipped parsley**
½ **teaspoon dried basil, crushed**
13 **fluid ounces (360ml) tinned semi-skimmed milk**
8 **ounces (225g) frozen peeled and deveined prawns**
3 **tablespoons cornflour**
3 **tablespoons water**
6 **ounces (175g) tinned crabmeat, flaked, drained, and cartilage removed**
½ **teaspoon salt**
⅛ **teaspoon pepper**

175 calories per serving

Prepare Chicken Stock (see photos 1–3, page 36). In a large saucepan combine Chicken Stock, carrots, celery, corn, parsley, and basil. Bring to boiling; reduce heat. Cover and simmer for 8 to 10 minutes or until vegetables are crisp-tender. Stir in milk and prawns, then return to boiling. Combine cornflour and water and stir into soup. Cook and stir until thickened and bubbly, then cook 2 minutes more. Stir in the crabmeat, salt, and pepper. Heat through. Ladle into soup bowls. Makes 6 servings.

Beefy Borscht

We took the best ingredients from several versions of borscht and created our own rich borscht.

32 **fluid ounces (900ml) Beef Stock (see recipe, page 37)**
   Cooking oil
1 **pound (450g) stewing steak, trimmed of separable fat and cut into ¾-inch (2cm) cubes**
1 **large turnip**
2 **medium beet roots *or* 16 ounces (450g) tinned beet roots, drained and cut into julienne strips**
1 **carrot**
¾ **teaspoon salt**
8 **ounces (225g) shredded cabbage**

150 calories per serving

Prepare Beef Stock (see photos 1–3, page 36). Coat the casserole dish with cooking oil. Cook meat in covered casserole over medium-high heat until meat is brown. Drain off fat.

Meanwhile, peel turnip, beet roots, if needed, and carrot. Cut turnip and beet roots, if needed, into thin, matchlike strips. Cut carrot into ¼-inch (½ cm) slices (see photo 1, page 90). Add Beef Stock, turnip, beet roots, carrot, salt, and ¼ teaspoon *pepper* to meat. Bring to boiling; reduce heat. Cover and simmer for 50 minutes. Stir in cabbage. Cover and cook 10 minutes more or until vegetables and meat are tender. Ladle into soup bowls. Serves 6.

Sausage and Cabbage Soup

We used smoked turkey sausage instead of pork sausage—it's lower in calories and just as flavoursome.

32   **fluid ounces (900ml) Beef Stock (see recipe, page 37)**
     Cooking oil
1   **large onion, chopped**
3   **ounces (75g) thinly sliced celery**
1   **ounce (25g) chopped green pepper**
1   **clove garlic, minced**
12   **ounces (350g) fully cooked smoked turkey sausage, cut into ½-inch (1cm) slices**
2   **medium potatoes, peeled and chopped (about 12 ounces [350g])**
2   **bay leaves**
½   **teaspoon salt**
½   **teaspoon caraway seed**
¼   **teaspoon pepper**
16   **ounces (450g) coarsely shredded cabbage**
     Parsley sprigs (optional)

215 calories per serving

Prepare Beef Stock (see photos 1–3, page 36). Coat a large saucepan with cooking oil. In the saucepan combine onion, celery, green pepper, and garlic. Cook and stir over medium heat until vegetables are tender.

Stir in Beef Stock, sausage, potatoes, bay leaves, salt, caraway seed, and pepper. Bring mixture to boiling; reduce heat. Cover and simmer for 10 to 15 minutes or until potatoes are nearly tender. Remove bay leaves. Stir in cabbage. Cook, covered, for 5 to 10 minutes more or until the cabbage is crisp-tender. Ladle into soup bowls. Top each serving with parsley, if desired. Makes 6 servings.

Vegetable-Tofu Soup

12   **fluid ounces (330ml) Chicken Stock (see recipe, page 36)**
1   **tablespoon minced dried onion**
¼   **teaspoon dried basil *or* oregano, crushed**
12   **ounces (350g) loose-pack frozen mixed vegetables**
10¾   **ounces (290g) tinned condensed cream of celery *or* cream of mushroom soup**
12   **fluid ounces (330ml) skimmed milk**
8   **ounces (225g) tofu (fresh bean curd), drained and cut into ½-inch (1cm) cubes**
3   **ounces (75g) grated processed cheese**

261 calories per serving

Prepare Chicken Stock (see photos 1–3, page 36). In a large saucepan combine Chicken Stock, onion, and basil or oregano. Bring to boiling. Stir in vegetables and return to boiling; reduce heat. Cover and simmer for 5 minutes. Stir in soup. Gradually add milk, then bring to boiling. Reduce heat. Add tofu and cheese and stir gently until cheese melts. Ladle into soup bowls. Makes 4 servings.

Clarifying Stock

Don't be alarmed if your home-made stock is cloudy even after straining. For a clear, rich-looking stock, you need to clarify it.

First, in a large saucepan stir together 2 fluid ounces (55ml) *cold water*, 1 *egg white*, and 1 *crushed eggshell*. Then, add the strained stock and bring it to boiling. Remove from the heat and let stand 5 minutes. Strain stock again through a colander or sieve lined with several layers of damp cheesecloth.

Elegant Poached Entrées

Tantalize your taste buds with these tempting entrées. Poaching (simmering food in a moderate amount of liquid) lends itself to low-calorie cooking. By using a liquid instead of cooking oil or fat, and the seasonings of your choice, you can keep calories under control. It doesn't matter if you prefer a fiery Mexican accent or a subtly sweet Hawaiian flavour. Simply change the character of the dish by varying the cooking liquid and seasonings.

Eggs Olé

Eggs Olé

4	6-inch (15cm) flour tortillas
2	large tomatoes, peeled, cored, and chopped
8	ounces (225g) tinned sieved tomatoes
4	ounces (110g) tinned green chilli peppers, rinsed, seeded, and chopped
2	teaspoons minced dried onion
¼	teaspoon dried oregano, crushed
5	ounces (150g) chopped cooked chicken *or* turkey
	Cooking oil
4	eggs

286 calories per serving

Brush one tortilla lightly with water to make it more pliable. Press it into an ovenproof 10-ounce (275g) casserole, shaping tortilla to fit the casserole (see photo 1). Repeat with remaining tortillas. Place casseroles in a shallow baking tin. Bake in a 350°F (180°C) gas mark 4 oven for 15 to 20 minutes or just until tortillas are crisp. Cool on a wire rack; remove tortillas.

For sauce, in a medium saucepan combine tomatoes, sieved tomatoes, chilli peppers, onion, and oregano. Bring to boiling; reduce heat. Boil gently, uncovered, for 10 minutes or until desired consistency. Add chicken or turkey, then heat through. Keep warm.

To poach eggs, coat a 10-inch (25.5cm) frying pan with cooking oil. Add enough water to half-fill the pan (see photo 2). Bring water to boiling; reduce heat to simmering. Break an egg into a sauce dish. Carefully slide egg into water (see photo 3). Repeat with remaining eggs so each has about equal space in the frying pan.

(For perfectly round poached eggs, place a metal egg ring in the simmering water. Slip egg into centre of the ring. As soon as egg white sets, remove the ring.) Smooth edges of eggs during cooking by using a spoon to gently pull away any strings of egg white (see photo 4). Simmer, uncovered, for 3 to 5 minutes or until eggs are desired doneness.

Spoon a scant 4 fluid ounces (110ml) of sauce into *each* tortilla bowl, then place an *egg* in *each* tortilla bowl (see photo 5). Salt, if desired. Top with remaining sauce. Makes 4 servings.

1 To make a tortilla bowl, brush the tortilla lightly with water to keep it from breaking or cracking. The slightly moist tortilla will be more pliable so you can shape it easily. Shape the tortilla in a ruffle to fit a 10-ounce (275g) casserole, as shown.

2 Pour enough water or other cooking liquid into the frying pan so that it is half full. This is usually about 1 inch (2.5cm) of liquid.

5 Lift the cooked eggs out of the poaching liquid with a slotted spoon, draining well. Carefully place each egg into a tortilla bowl atop the sauce mixture.

3 Carefully slide the egg into the simmering liquid, holding the lip of the dish as close to the liquid as possible.

4 To make the eggs more attractive, use a slotted spoon to pull away any strings of the egg white that form while the eggs are cooking.

Hawaiian Chicken

Pineapple canned with natural juice is lower in calories than pineapple in syrup.

2 whole medium chicken breasts (about 1½ pounds (700g) total), halved lengthwise
8 ounces (225g) tinned pineapple chunks *or* pieces in juice
3 fluid ounces (20ml) orange juice
2 tablespoons soy sauce
½ teaspoon minced dried onion
2 teaspoons cornflour
2 teaspoons cold water

191 calories per serving

Remove and discard skin from chicken. Drain pineapple, reserving liquid. In a 10-inch (25.5cm) frying pan combine the reserved liquid, orange juice, soy sauce, and onion (see photo 2, page 42). Bring to boiling. Add chicken, then reduce heat. Cover and simmer for 25 to 30 minutes or until chicken is tender, turning once. Transfer chicken to a dish; keep warm.

For sauce, stir together cornflour and water (see photo 4, page 25). Add to cooking liquid. Cook and stir until thickened and bubbly. Add pineapple, then cook and stir 2 minutes more. Spoon sauce over chicken. Makes 4 servings.

Zesty Chicken

2 whole medium chicken breasts (about 1½ pounds (700g) total), halved lengthwise
8 fluid ounces (220ml) vegetable juice cocktail
1 ounce (25g) chopped green pepper
2 ounces (50g) chopped onion
1 clove garlic, minced
½ teaspoon dried oregano, crushed
Dash bottled hot pepper sauce
1 tablespoon cornflour
1 tablespoon cold water

172 calories per serving

Remove and discard skin from chicken. In a 10-inch (25.5cm) frying pan combine vegetable cocktail, green pepper, onion, garlic, oregano, and pepper sauce (see photo 2, page 42). Bring to boiling. Add chicken, then reduce heat. Cover and simmer for 25 to 30 minutes or until chicken is tender. Transfer to a dish and keep warm.

For sauce, stir together cornflour and cold water (see photo 4, page 25). Add to cooking liquid in frying pan. Cook and stir until thickened and bubbly, then cook and stir 2 minutes more. Spoon sauce over chicken. Makes 4 servings.

Poached Halibut in Tangy Lime Sauce

4 4-ounce (125g each) fresh *or* frozen small halibut steaks
½ teaspoon finely grated lime peel
3 tablespoons lime juice
¼ teaspoon dried rosemary, crushed
4 ounces (125g) natural low-fat yogurt
1 tablespoon plain flour

180 calories per serving

Thaw fish, if frozen. In a 10-inch (25.5cm) frying pan combine lime peel, lime juice, rosemary, 8 fluid ounces (220ml) *water,* ¼ teaspoon *salt,* and ⅛ teaspoon *pepper* (see photo 2, page 42). Add fish and bring to boiling; reduce heat. Cover and simmer for 8 to 10 minutes or until fish flakes easily with a fork (see photo 3, page 85). Transfer fish to a serving dish, leaving cooking liquid in the pan. Keep fish warm.

For sauce, bring cooking liquid to boiling. Boil 5 minutes or until reduced to 4 fluid ounces (110ml). Reduce heat. In a small bowl combine yogurt and flour. Stir about *half* of the hot mixture into yogurt mixture, then return all to hot mixture. Cook and stir until thickened and bubbly, then cook and stir 1 minute more. Spoon sauce over fish. Garnish with lime slices and parsley, if desired. Makes 4 servings.

Poached Fish with Lemon-Dill Sauce

If you don't have a fish poacher, use a large roasting tin. Wrap the fish in cheesecloth, then lay the fish on two wide strips of doubled foil in the tin. (The strips should be long enough to allow you to lift the fish.) When the fish is cooked, use the foil strips to remove the fish from the roasting tin.

3   pounds (1kg350g) fresh *or* frozen dressed whiting *or* cod
8   fluid ounces (220ml) water
8   fluid ounces (220ml) dry white wine
½   teaspoon salt
⅛   teaspoon pepper
½   lemon, cut into wedges
1   bay leaf
1   tablespoon plain flour
4   ounces (110g) soured cream
1   teaspoon fresh snipped dill *or* ¼ teaspoon dried dill

253 calories per serving

Thaw fish, if frozen. Place fish on a large piece of cheesecloth, then fold cloth over fish. Place on a rack in a poaching tin. Add water, wine, salt, and pepper (see photo 2, page 42). Squeeze lemon wedges over fish, then add lemon wedges and bay leaf to poaching liquid. Bring to boiling; reduce heat. Cover and simmer for 25 to 30 minutes or until fish flakes easily with a fork (see photo 3, page 85). Remove fish from pan and keep warm. Strain and reserve 4 fluid ounces (110ml) of the cooking liquid.

For sauce, in a small saucepan stir flour into soured cream. Stir in reserved liquid and dill. Cook and stir until thickened and bubbly, then cook and stir 1 minute more.

Pull cloth away from fish and discard, then remove and discard skin. Transfer fish to a serving dish using two metal spatulas. Top with some of the sauce. Serves 6.

Poached Eggs with Prawn Sauce

1   tablespoon butter *or* margarine
2   teaspoons cornflour
⅛   teaspoon dried tarragon, crushed
    Dash pepper
5   fluid ounces (140ml) skimmed milk
4½   ounces (125g) tinned prawns, rinsed and drained
10   ounces (275g) frozen chopped spinach
    Cooking oil
4   eggs
2   tablespoons grated Swiss cheese

194 calories per serving

For sauce, in a small saucepan melt butter or margarine. Stir in cornflour, tarragon, and pepper. Add milk all at once. Cook and stir over medium heat until thickened and bubbly, then cook and stir 2 minutes more. Stir in prawns and heat through. Keep sauce warm.

Cook spinach according to package directions. Meanwhile, to poach eggs, coat a 10-inch (25.5cm) frying pan with cooking oil. Add enough water to half-fill the pan, about 1 inch (2.5cm) (see photo 2, page 42). Bring to boiling. Reduce heat to simmering. Break an egg into a sauce dish. Carefully slide egg into water, holding lip of the dish as close to water as possible (see photo 3, page 43). Repeat with remaining eggs so each has about equal space in the frying pan. (For perfectly round eggs, place a metal egg ring in the simmering water. Slip egg into centre of the ring. As soon as egg white sets, remove the ring.) Smooth edges of eggs during cooking by using a spoon to gently pull away any floating strings of egg white (see photo 4, page 43). Simmer, uncovered, for 3 to 5 minutes or until eggs reach desired doneness.

Thoroughly drain spinach. Spoon spinach onto four individual plates. Lift eggs out of water using a slotted spoon and place an egg atop spinach on each plate. Season eggs lightly with salt. Spoon sauce over eggs. Sprinkle each serving with cheese. Makes 4 servings.

Tantalizing Grilled Meats

Finding a quick way to prepare dazzling dishes is important with today's busy life-styles. That's where grilling comes in—it's fast *and easy.*

Grilling offers another bonus—it uses no added fat. And, the fat that cooks out of the food is left behind in the grill pan.

Lamb Chops with Lemon-Mustard Sauce

Lamb Chops with Lemon-Mustard Sauce

Elegant enough for company; low-calorie enough to please everyone.

4   **gigot lamb chops, cut ¾ inch (2cm) thick (1¼ pounds [560g] total)**
½   **teaspoon lemon pepper**
½   **teaspoon mustard powder**
3   **fluid ounces (80ml) chicken broth**
1   **teaspoon cornflour**
2   **tablespoons French mustard**
¼   **teaspoon grated lemon peel**
1   **tablespoon lemon juice**
⅛   **teaspoon dried oregano, crushed**
1   **clove garlic, minced**
    Fresh herb sprigs (optional)

142 calories per serving

Trim separable fat from chops (see photo 1, page 24). In a small bowl combine lemon pepper and mustard powder, then rub mixture into chops (see photo 1). Place chops on an unheated rack in a grill pan. Grill 3 to 4 inches (7.5 to 10cm) from the heat for 5 to 6 minutes (see photo 2). Turn chops (see photo 3). Grill 3 to 4 minutes more or until desired doneness (see photo 4).

Meanwhile, for sauce, in a small saucepan combine chicken broth and cornflour. Stir in French mustard, lemon peel, lemon juice, oregano, and garlic. Cook and stir until thickened and bubbly, then cook and stir 2 minutes more. Serve sauce over chops. Garnish with herbs, if desired. Makes 4 servings.

1 Rub the herb mixture into both sides of each chop with your fingers.

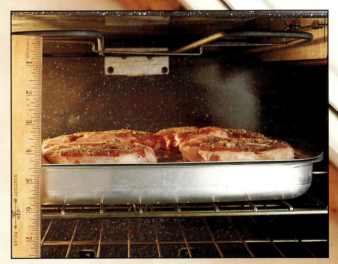

2 Place the chops on an unheated rack in a grill pan so that the surface of the chops is 3 to 4 inches (7.5 to 10cm) from the heat source, as shown. Usually the door of an electric cooker needs to be ajar while the grill is in use, but the door on a gas cooker is closed. Read the manufacturer's directions for your cooker to be sure.

3 Use tongs or a metal spatula instead of a fork to carefully turn each chop, as shown. Forks pierce meat, causing the loss of flavoursome juices.

4 Test the chops to see if ready by making a small slit in the centre of one of the chops. A medium-done chop will have a pink centre; a well-done chop will be grey. For medium-cooked, allow 6 minutes per side for ¾-inch (2cm) chops.

Pineapple-Ham Kababs

¾ **pound (350g) fully cooked boneless ham**
8 **ounces (225g) tinned pineapple slices in juice**
1 **medium green pepper, cut into squares**
1 **tablespoon honey**
½ **teaspoon cornflour**
¼ **teaspoon ground cinnamon**

204 calories per serving

Trim separable fat from ham (see photo 1, page 24). Cut ham into ¾-inch (2cm) cubes. Drain pineapple slices, reserving juice. Quarter pineapple slices. On four long or eight short skewers alternately thread ham, pineapple, and green pepper.

For sauce, in a small saucepan combine reserved pineapple juice, honey, cornflour, and cinnamon. Cook and stir until slightly thickened and bubbly, then cook and stir 2 minutes more. Baste kababs generously with some sauce.

Place kababs on an unheated rack in a grill pan. Grill kababs 4 inches (10cm) from heat for 5 minutes (see photo 2, page 48). Brush occasionally with sauce. Turn kababs and grill about 5 minutes more, brushing with sauce occasionally. Brush with remaining sauce before serving. Makes 4 servings.

Orange-Ginger Lobster

To clean your grill pan more easily, let it soak for a few minutes in hot soapy water.

4 **8-ounce (225g each) frozen lobster tails**
½ **teaspoon grated orange peel**
4 **fluid ounces (110ml) orange juice**
1 **teaspoon cornflour**
⅛ **teaspoon ground ginger**
1 **tablespoon butter *or* margarine**

150 calories per serving

Partially thaw lobster. Use a sharp, heavy knife to cut through centre of hard top shell. Cut through meat, but not through undershell. Pull tail open, butterfly-style, so meat is on top.

Place tails on an unheated rack in a grill pan, cut side up. Grill about 5 inches (13cm) from the heat for 12 to 15 minutes (see photo 2, page 48). Lobster should lose its translucency and flake easily when tested with a fork (see photo 3, page 85). Loosen meat from shell by inserting a fork between shell and meat.

Meanwhile, for dipping sauce, in a medium saucepan combine orange peel, orange juice, cornflour, and ginger. Cook and stir until thickened and bubbly, then cook and stir 2 minutes more. Stir in butter or margarine until melted. Serve sauce with lobster. Makes 4 servings.

Cheese-Stuffed Burgers

Mozzarella cheese has only 79 calories in 1 ounce (25g), but you also can use Swiss cheese (105 calories) or cheddar cheese (113 calories).

1 beaten egg
2 tablespoons fine dry bread crumbs
1 tablespoon water
¼ teaspoon garlic salt
¼ teaspoon dried thyme, crushed
  Dash pepper
1 pound (450g) lean minced beef
1 ounce (25g) grated mozzarella cheese
1 tablespoon snipped parsley
1 small tomato, thinly sliced

245 calories per serving

In a medium bowl combine egg, bread crumbs, water, garlic salt, thyme, and pepper. Add beef and mix well. Shape beef mixture into eight ¼-inch-thick (½cm) patties.

In a small bowl combine cheese and parsley. Spoon cheese mixture onto *four* patties. Top with remaining patties, then press edges to seal.

Place burgers on an unheated rack in a grill pan. Grill 3 inches (7.5cm) from the heat for 4 minutes (see photo 2, page 48). Turn patties with a metal spatula (see photo 3, page 49). Broil 4 to 5 minutes more or until cooked to suit. Top burgers with tomato slices. Makes 4 servings.

South Seas Steak Pinwheels

Kiwi fruit is lemon-shaped with soft, fuzzy brown skin and delicate green fruit.

¾ pound (350g) boneless chuck steak, cut ½ inch (1cm) thick
1 papaya, peeled and seeded
1 small banana, finely chopped
2 teaspoons lemon juice
  Dash ground nutmeg
1 kiwi fruit, peeled and cut into thin slices

159 calories per serving

Trim separable fat from meat (see photo 1, page 24). Pound to ⅛-inch (3mm) thickness (see photo 2, page 114). Sprinkle with salt and pepper. Finely chop enough papaya to weigh 4 ounces (110g). Slice the remainder for garnish and set sliced papaya aside. In a small bowl combine chopped papaya, banana, lemon juice, and nutmeg. Spread fruit mixture over meat. Roll up Swiss-roll style. Secure with wooden toothpicks. Cut crosswise into four slices.

Place meat on an unheated rack in a grill pan. Grill meat 3 to 4 inches (7.5 to 10cm) from the heat for 5 to 6 minutes (see photo 2, page 48). Carefully turn meat with a metal spatula (see photo 3, page 49). Grill 4 to 5 minutes more or until cooked to suit. Garnish meat with kiwi fruit and sliced papaya. Makes 4 servings.

Perfect Pasta

Now it's easy to eat great-tasting pasta dishes while watching your weight. The key to slimming success is low-calorie sauces.

   Surprisingly, pasta isn't the calorie culprit. It's the rich, high-calorie sauces that make pasta dishes off-limits to dieters. Try any of the exciting recipes in this section and you can treat yourself to pasta as often as you please.

Vegetable Carbonara

Vegetable Carbonara

Often, green noodles are called spinach noodles on the packet. If you can't find them at the supermarket, substitute regular noodles.

4 ounces (110g) green noodles
8 ounces (225g) tofu (fresh bean curd)
1 carrot
2 fluid ounces (55ml) water
1 medium courgette, halved lengthwise and sliced ¼ inch (½cm) thick
3 ounces (75g) sliced fresh mushrooms
1 ounce (25g) snipped parsley
¼ teaspoon salt
¼ teaspoon dried basil, crushed
2 slightly beaten eggs
2 tablespoons grated Parmesan cheese

245 calories per serving

Cook noodles according to packet directions; test for doneness (see photo 1). Drain noodles and keep warm (see photo 2). Meanwhile, drain tofu (bean curd). Wrap tofu in a double thickness of cheesecloth or kitchen paper, pressing gently to extract as much moisture as possible. Cut into ½-inch (1cm) cubes (see photo 3).

Cut carrot into thin, matchlike strips (julienne strips). In a 10-inch (25.5cm) frying pan bring carrot and water to boiling; reduce heat to medium-high. Cover and cook for 3 minutes. Stir in tofu, courgette, mushrooms, parsley, salt, and basil (see photo 4). Cover and cook about 7 minutes more or till courgette is tender. Drain.

In a small bowl combine eggs and cheese. Add hot noodles to the frying pan and toss with vegetables, then remove frying pan from heat. Immediately add egg mixture to the pan, then toss well to coat (see photo 5). Serves 4.

1 Near the end of the cooking time, test the pasta frequently for doneness by cutting with a fork or biting into a piece. When it's done, the pasta should be tender but still slightly firm. Italians call this *al dente* (to the tooth).

2 When the pasta tests done, immediately transfer it to a colander over a sink and drain, being careful to avoid the hot steam. Give it a couple of shakes to help remove excess moisture. Keep the pasta warm after draining by placing the colander over a pot of hot water. Or, return the pasta to the pot and cover. Place the pot in a warm oven for a while.

3 After thoroughly draining tofu, use a serrated knife to make lengthwise cuts about ½ inch (1cm) apart. Then, cut crosswise to make cubes.

4 Add the tofu cubes, courgette, mushrooms, parsley, salt, and basil to the frying pan with the cooked carrots. Push the vegetables off the cutting board and into the pan with a spatula so the hot liquid does not splash and hit your arm.

5 Toss the egg and Parmesan cheese mixture with the hot mixture in the frying pan immediately, as shown. A wooden pasta fork and spatula work particularly well. Or, use two spoons. This tossing distributes the egg and cheese mixture, evenly coating the pasta and vegetables. Heat from the hot mixture will quickly cook the eggs.

Fettuccine with Clam Sauce

6 ounces (175g) fettuccine, green noodles, *or* spaghetti
13 to 15 ounces (375 to 425g) tinned whole clams in brine, minced
4 ounces (110g) thinly sliced carrots
14 fluid ounces (385ml) skimmed milk
1½ ounces (40g) cornflour
3 sliced spring onions
2 ounces (50g) grated Swiss cheese
1 ounce (25g) chopped pimento
¼ teaspoon salt
¼ teaspoon dried dill
Dash pepper
Snipped parsley (optional)

238 calories per serving

Cook fettuccine, green noodles, or spaghetti according to packet directions or to taste (see photo 1, page 54). Drain the pasta and keep warm (see photo 2, page 54).

Meanwhile, for sauce, drain clams, reserving liquid. Set clams aside. In a large saucepan combine reserved liquid and carrots. Bring to boiling; reduce heat. Cover and simmer for 6 to 8 minutes or till tender. Stir together milk and cornflour (see photo 4, page 25). Add all at once to carrot mixture. Add spring onion. Cook and stir till thickened and bubbly, then cook and stir 2 minutes more.

Stir in clams, cheese, pimento, salt, dill, and pepper, then heat through. Ladle clam sauce over pasta on a serving dish. Garnish with parsley, if desired. Makes 6 servings.

Scallops Italian

¾ pound (350g) fresh *or* frozen scallops
4 ounces (110g) linguine *or* spaghetti
Cooking oil
1 ounce (25g) sliced celery
2 ounces (50g) chopped onion
1 clove garlic, minced
8 ounces (225g) tinned tomatoes, cut up
8 fluid ounces (220ml) tinned sieved tomatoes
3 ounces (75g) tinned sliced mushrooms, drained
¼ teaspoon dried rosemary, crushed
¼ teaspoon dried thyme, crushed
⅛ teaspoon salt
2 tablespoons snipped parsley
4 teaspoons cornflour
1 tablespoon cold water

257 calories per serving

Thaw scallops, if frozen. Cut any large scallops in half and set aside. Cook linguine or spaghetti according to packet directions; test for doneness (see photo 1, page 54). Drain pasta and keep warm (see photo 2, page 54).

Meanwhile, coat a medium saucepan with cooking oil. For sauce, in the saucepan cook celery, onion, and garlic until onion is tender. Stir in *undrained* tomatoes, sieved tomatoes, mushrooms, rosemary, thyme, and salt. Bring to boiling; add scallops and parsley. Return to boiling; reduce heat. Cover and simmer for 4 to 5 minutes or till scallops are nearly opaque.

Combine cornflour and water (see photo 4, page 25). Stir cornflour mixture into tomato mixture. Cook and stir till thickened and bubbly, then cook and stir 2 minutes more. Serve sauce over hot linguine or spaghetti on individual plates. Makes 4 servings.

Beefy Vegetable-Sauced Pasta

4	ounces (110g) fine *or* medium noodles
¾	pound (350g) lean minced beef
2	ounces (50g) chopped onion
1	ounce (25g) chopped green pepper
5	ounces (150g) thinly sliced cauliflower florets
10½	ounces (285g) tinned tomato puree
8	ounces (225g) tinned tomatoes, cut up
1	ounce (25g) snipped parsley
1	teaspoon dried oregano, crushed
½	teaspoon salt
¼	teaspoon dried basil, crushed
⅛	teaspoon garlic powder

305 calories per serving

Cook noodles according to packet directions or to taste (see photo 1, page 54). Drain noodles and keep warm (see photo 2, page 54).

Meanwhile, for sauce, in a 10-inch (25.5cm) frying pan cook beef, onion, and green pepper till meat is brown and vegetables are tender, then drain off fat (see photo 1, page 30). Stir in cauliflower, tomato puree, *undrained* tomatoes, parsley, oregano, salt, basil, and garlic powder. Bring to boiling; reduce heat. Cover and simmer for 15 to 20 minutes or till the cauliflower is crisp-tender. Ladle sauce over noodles on a serving dish. Makes 4 servings.

White Lasagne

Enjoy this Northern Italian-style lasagne that features a rich white sauce in place of the traditional Southern-style tomato sauce.

4	ounces (110g) lasagne noodles (6 noodles)
10	ounces (275g) frozen chopped broccoli
16	fluid ounces (440ml) skimmed milk
2	tablespoons cornflour
1	tablespoon minced dried onion
8	ounces (225g) diced fully cooked ham
½	teaspoon Italian seasoning, crushed
8	ounces (225g) low-fat cottage cheese
6	ounces (175g) grated mozzarella cheese

284 calories per serving

Cook lasagne noodles according to packet directions or to taste (see photo 1, page 54). Drain noodles (see photo 2, page 54). Rinse noodles with cold water.

Meanwhile, cook broccoli according to packet directions; drain well. Set aside. For sauce, in a medium saucepan combine milk, cornflour, and onion. Cook and stir until thickened and bubbly, then cook and stir 2 minutes more. Stir in broccoli, ham, and Italian seasoning.

Place *2 tablespoons* of the sauce on the bottom of a 10x6x2-inch (25.5x15x5cm) baking dish, then spread evenly. Place *two* of the lasagne noodles in baking dish. Spread noodles with *half* of the cottage cheese. Add *one-third* of sauce and mozzarella. Repeat noodle, cottage cheese, sauce, and mozzarella layers, then top with remaining noodles, sauce, and mozzarella.

Bake in a 375°F (190°C) gas mark 5 oven for 30 to 35 minutes or until heated through. (*Or*, assemble and chill for up to 24 hours. Bake 45 to 50 minutes or until heated through.) Let stand 10 minutes before serving. Makes 6 servings.

Delectable Microwave Entrées

For a fast, efficient way to create spectacular low-calorie meals, put your microwave to work. Relish the flavours of piquant Pepper Steak, Quick Beef Stew, or Hot Turkey Salad. They're proof that the microwave oven can do some serious figuring in your diet plans.

Pepper Steak

Pepper Steak

¾ **pound (350g) chuck *or* blade bone
    steak**
1 **teaspoon grated root ginger**
2 **tablespoons soy sauce**
2 **tablespoons dry sherry**
2 **teaspoons cornflour**
1 **teaspoon instant beef bouillon
    granules**
1 **large green pepper, cut into strips**
1 **small tomato, cut into thin wedges**
10½ **ounces (285g) hot cooked noodles**

229 calories per serving

Trim separable fat from meat (see photo 1,
page 24). Partially freeze meat. Thinly slice
meat across the grain into strips (see photo 1).
Place in a 3½-pint (2 litre) nonmetal casserole.
Micro-cook, covered, on 100% power (HIGH)
for 4 to 5 minutes or until no longer pink, stirring twice (see photo 2).

Grate ginger (see photo 3). Mix ginger, soy
sauce, sherry, cornflour, bouillon granules, and
2 tablespoons *cold water*. Stir into beef. Stir in
green pepper. Micro-cook, uncovered, on 100%
power (HIGH) for 4 to 5 minutes or until thickened and bubbly, stirring *every* minute. Stir in
tomato (see photo 4). Micro-cook, covered, on
100% power (HIGH) for 1 minute or until hot.
Serve over noodles. Makes 4 servings.

1 Thinly slice the meat
by holding a sharp
knife at a slight angle to
the cutting surface. Slice
across the grain of the
meat, making thin slices
2 to 3 inches (5 to
7.5cm) long.

The meat is easier to
slice when it's partially
frozen. Allow 45 to 60
minutes for the meat to
partially freeze.

2 During the cooking
time, stir the meat
two or three times. Use
a folding motion to
move the pieces of food
on the outside of the
dish to the centre and
the pieces of food in the
centre of the dish to the
outside. This helps en-
sure even cooking.

3 To grate root ginger, hold a piece of unpeeled root ginger at a 45-degree angle. Rub it across a fine grating surface, as shown. Or, use a ginger grater like the one on the cutting board. Wrap the unused root ginger in kitchen paper and refrigerate.

4 Gently stir in the tomato wedges. These are stirred in at the last minute so they just heat through, but don't lose their shape.

Hot Turkey Salad

¾ pound (350g) boneless turkey fillets *or* steaks
3 tablespoons cold water
3 tablespoons tarragon vinegar
2 tablespoons chopped onion
1 tablespoon sugar
1 teaspoon cornflour
½ teaspoon salt
¼ teaspoon dry mustard
¼ teaspoon celery seed
Dash pepper
8 ounces (225g) torn fresh spinach
8 ounces (225g) shredded cabbage
2 ounces (50g) sliced radishes
2 hard-cooked eggs, sliced

154 calories per serving

With a sharp knife slice turkey into bite-size strips. Place turkey in a large nonmetal casserole. Micro-cook turkey, covered, on 100% power (HIGH) for 3 to 4 minutes or until turkey is almost done, stirring two or three times (see photo 2, page 60). Remove turkey from the casserole and drain well.

For dressing, in the same casserole combine water, vinegar, onion, sugar, cornflour, salt, mustard, celery seed, and pepper. Micro-cook, uncovered, on 100% power (HIGH) for 2 minutes or until mixture is thickened and bubbly, stirring every 30 seconds.

Return turkey to casserole. Add spinach, cabbage, and radishes. Toss to coat with hot dressing. Micro-cook, uncovered, on 100% power (HIGH) for 2 minutes or until heated through, stirring once. Carefully fold in eggs. Makes 4 servings.

Quick Beef Stew

4 cubed beefsteaks (1 pound [450g])
10¾ ounces (290g) tinned condensed tomato soup
4 fluid ounces (110ml) water
1 medium onion, cut into 8 wedges
1 teaspoon instant beef bouillon granules
1 teaspoon dried savory, crushed
⅛ teaspoon garlic powder
⅛ teaspoon pepper
2 ounces (50g) sliced courgette
8¾ ounces (240g) tinned sweet corn, drained

249 calories per serving

With a sharp knife slice steaks into bite-size strips. Place meat in a medium nonmetal casserole. Micro-cook meat, covered, on 100% power (HIGH) for 3 to 4 minutes or until meat is no longer pink, stirring two or three times (see photo 2, page 60). Drain.

Stir in soup, water, onion, bouillon granules, savory, garlic powder, and pepper, then add courgette and corn. Micro-cook, covered, on 100% power (HIGH) for 13 minutes more or until courgette is tender. Ladle mixture into soup bowls. Makes 4 servings.

Attention, Microwave Owners!

The microwave timings in this book were tested using countertop microwave ovens with 600 to 700 watts of cooking power. The cooking times are approximate because microwave ovens vary by manufacturer.

Pork Strips in Pineapple Sauce

1 pound (450g) lean boneless pork
1 clove garlic, minced
9 ounces (250g) frozen French beans
4 ounces (110g) frozen crinkle-cut
   carrots
8 ounces (225g) tinned pineapple pieces
   in juice
1 tablespoon cornflour
½ teaspoon instant beef bouillon
   granules
⅛ teaspoon ground cinnamon

245 calories per serving

Trim separable fat from meat (see photo 1, page 24). Partially freeze meat. Thinly slice meat across the grain into bite-size strips (see photo 1, page 60). Place meat and garlic in a medium nonmetal casserole. Micro-cook meat mixture, covered, on 100% power (HIGH) for 5 minutes or until meat is no longer pink, stirring two or three times (see photo 2, page 60).

Add beans and carrots to the meat mixture. Micro-cook, covered, on 100% power (HIGH) 7 to 9 minutes more or until pork is cooked and vegetables are tender, stirring three or four times. Drain off cooking liquid and reserve.

Drain pineapple, reserving juice. Add enough of the cooking liquid to reserved pineapple juice to measure 6 fluid ounces (165ml) of liquid. In a nonmetal bowl combine pineapple juice mixture, cornflour, bouillon granules, and cinnamon. Micro-cook, uncovered, on 100% power (HIGH) for 2 to 3 minutes or until thickened and bubbly, stirring every 30 seconds.

Stir pineapple and pineapple juice mixture into meat mixture and mix well. Micro-cook, uncovered, on 100% power (HIGH) for 1 to 2 minutes or until heated through. Makes 4 servings.

Easy Chop Suey

Make this dish even easier by substituting warmed chow mein noodles for the rice.

¾ pound (350g) lean boneless pork
5 ounces (150g) sliced celery
3 spring onions, sliced into 1-inch
   (2.5cm) pieces
6 fluid ounces (165ml) cold water
4 teaspoons cornflour
1 tablespoon soy sauce
1 teaspoon instant chicken bouillon
   granules
16 ounces (450g) tinned bean sprouts,
   drained, *or* 16 ounces (450g) fresh
   bean sprouts
4 ounces (110g) tinned sliced
   mushrooms, drained
2 tablespoons sliced pimento
2 pounds (1kg125g) hot cooked rice

245 calories per serving

Trim separable fat from meat (see photo 1, page 24). Partially freeze meat. Thinly slice meat across the grain into bite-size strips (see photo 1, page 60). Place meat in a medium nonmetal casserole. Micro-cook meat, covered, on 100% power (HIGH) for 4 minutes or until meat is no longer pink, stirring two or three times (see photo 2, page 60).

Add celery and onions to meat. Micro-cook, covered, on 100% power (HIGH) about 4 minutes more or until celery is crisp-tender, stirring twice. In a small bowl stir together water, cornflour, soy sauce, and bouillon granules. Stir mixture into meat mixture. Micro-cook, uncovered, on 100% power (HIGH) for 4 minutes or until thickened and bubbly, stirring twice.

Stir in sprouts, mushrooms, and pimento. Micro-cook, uncovered, on 100% power (HIGH) about 2 minutes more or until heated through. Serve over rice. Makes 4 servings.

Succulent Baked Poultry

Choosy dieters opt for chicken because it's low in calories, but oh, so flavoursome. Cut chicken calories even more by selecting the leaner white pieces such as the breast and wings over the higher-calorie dark pieces. Remove the skin to slash 20 more calories per piece. Then bake until delicately browned and fork tender.

Carrot-Stuffed Chicken Rolls

Chicken Rolls

2 **whole medium chicken breasts**
   (about 1½ pounds [700g] total)
4 **small carrots**
   Lemon pepper
2 **teaspoons butter** *or* **margarine**
3 **tablespoons dry white wine**
2 **tablespoons water**
¼ **teaspoon celery salt**
5 **ounces (150g) thinly sliced celery**
1 **tablespoon cold water**
2 **teaspoons cornflour**

214 calories per serving

Place one chicken breast on a cutting board, skin side up. Pull skin away from meat, then discard skin. Bone breast and pound halves (see photos 1–2). Repeat with remaining chicken. Cut each carrot into eight sticks (see photo 3). In a medium saucepan cook carrots, covered, in a small amount of boiling water for 5 minutes; drain. Sprinkle chicken lightly with lemon pepper, then dot with butter or margarine. Place eight carrot sticks on each chicken piece and roll chicken around carrots (see photo 4).

Place rolls, seam side down, in an 8x3x2-inch (20x20x5cm) baking dish. In a bowl combine wine, 2 tablespoons water, and celery salt, then pour over chicken. Cover and bake in a 350°F (180°C) gas mark 4 oven for 30 to 35 minutes or until tender. Remove chicken and keep warm.

Measure pan juices, then add water to equal 6 fluid ounces (165ml) liquid. In a saucepan cook celery, covered, in the liquid for 3 minutes or until tender. Combine 1 tablespoon cold water and cornflour; stir into celery mixture. Cook and stir until thickened and bubbly, then cook and stir 2 minutes more. Serve sauce over chicken. Makes 4 servings.

1 Place the skinned whole chicken breast on a cutting board, meat side up. Starting to one side of the breastbone, use a thin, sharp knife to cut the meat away from the bone. Cut as close to the bone as possible, as shown. Press the flat side of the knife against the rib bones and cut using a sawing motion. Gently pull the meat away from the rib bones as you cut. Repeat on the other side.

2 Place a chicken breast half between two pieces of clear clingfilm. Gently pound the chicken with the smooth side of a meat mallet. Work from the centre to the edges to form a rectangle ⅛ inch (3mm) thick.

3 With a sharp knife cut each of the carrots in half lengthwise. Cut each in half again to make four carrot sticks. Now cut each carrot stick in half again to make eight short, thin carrot sticks.

4 Place eight of the cooked carrot sticks across the centre of each chicken breast. Roll up the chicken Swiss-roll style around the carrot sticks. Press edges of chicken together with your fingers.

Ham-Filled Chicken Rolls

2 **whole medium chicken breasts (about 1½ pounds [700g] total)**
3 **tablespoons reduced-oil salad dressing**
4 **ounces (110g) boiled ham, thinly sliced**
1 **ounce (25g) toasted wheat germ**
2 **tablespoons snipped parsley**
1 **beaten egg**

267 calories per serving

Place one chicken breast on a cutting board, skin side up. Pull the skin away from the meat, then discard skin. Bone breast and pound halves (see photos 1–2, pages 66–67). Repeat with the remaining chicken breast.

Spread each chicken piece with about 2 teaspoons of salad dressing, then add a ham slice. Starting from the short side, fold in sides and roll up Swiss-roll style, pressing roll shut (see photo 4, page 67). Repeat with remaining chicken.

In a bowl combine wheat germ and parsley. Dip chicken in beaten egg, then roll in wheat germ and parsley mixture. Place chicken in an 8x8x2-inch (20x20x5cm) baking dish. Bake in a 350°F (180°C) gas mark 4 oven for 30 to 35 minutes or till chicken is tender. Makes 4 servings.

Chicken Parmesan

3 **whole medium chicken breasts (about 2¼ pounds [1kg10g] total)**
1½ **ounces (40g) grated Parmesan cheese**
¼ **teaspoon Italian seasoning, crushed**
2 **sliced spring onions**
1 **tablespoon butter *or* margarine**
1 **tablespoon plain flour**
4 **fluid ounces (110ml) skimmed milk**
5 **ounces (150g) frozen chopped spinach, thawed and drained**
1 **tablespoon chopped pimento**

206 calories per serving

Place one chicken breast on a cutting board, skin side up. Pull the skin away from the meat, then discard skin. Bone chicken breast (see photo 1, page 66). Repeat with remaining breasts.

In a small mixing bowl combine Parmesan cheese and Italian seasoning. Roll chicken pieces in cheese mixture to coat lightly; set remaining cheese mixture aside.

Arrange pieces in an 8x8x2-inch (20x20x5cm) baking dish. In a small saucepan cook onion in hot butter or margarine till tender but not brown. Stir in flour, then add milk all at once. Cook and stir till thickened and bubbly; stir in drained spinach and pimento. Spoon spinach mixture over chicken and sprinkle with remaining cheese mixture. Bake, uncovered, in a 350°F (180°C) gas mark 4 oven for 30 to 35 minutes or till tender. Makes 6 servings.

Curried Pinwheels

Apple, raisins, coconut, curry, and peanuts add zesty Indian flavour.

2   **whole medium chicken breasts (about 1½ pounds [700g] total)**
1   **medium apple, cored and finely chopped**
1   **ounce (25g) raisins**
2   **tablespoons coconut**
6   **fluid ounces (165ml) hot water**
1   **teaspoon curry powder**
½   **teaspoon instant chicken bouillon granules**
1   **tablespoon cold water**
2   **teaspoons cornflour**
1   **tablespoon chopped peanuts**

225 calories per serving

Place one chicken breast on a cutting board, skin side up. Pull the skin away from the meat, then discard skin. Bone breast and pound halves (see photos 1–2, pages 66–67) Repeat with the remaining chicken breast.

In a small mixing bowl combine apple, raisins, and coconut. Spoon mixture onto chicken breast halves. Starting from a short side, roll up Swiss-roll style (see photo 4, page 67). Place chicken, seam side down, in an 8x3x2-inch (20x20x5cm) baking dish. In a small bowl combine hot water, curry powder, and bouillon granules, then pour over chicken.

Bake, covered, in a 350°F (180°C) gas mark 4 oven for 30 to 35 minutes or until chicken is tender. Transfer chicken to a serving dish; cover with foil to keep warm. For sauce, strain cooking juices, reserving 4 fluid ounces (110ml). In a small saucepan combine cold water and cornflour; add reserved cooking juices. Cook and stir until bubbly, then cook and stir 2 minutes more. To serve, cut each chicken roll into four slices. Serve sauce over slices and sprinkle with peanuts. Makes 4 servings.

Brandied Tarragon Chicken

2   **whole medium chicken breasts (about 1½ pounds [700g] total)**
2   **fluid ounces (55ml) brandy**
2½   **ounces (60g) tinned sliced mushrooms**
1   **teaspoon snipped fresh tarragon *or* ¼ teaspoon dried tarragon, crushed**
¼   **teaspoon salt**
¼   **teaspoon pepper**
    Sprigs of fresh tarragon (optional)

217 calories per serving

Place one chicken breast on a cutting board, skin side up. Pull the skin away from the meat, then discard skin. Bone breast (see photo 1, page 66). Repeat with the remaining chicken breast.

In a small mixing bowl combine brandy, *undrained* mushrooms, tarragon, salt, and pepper. Place chicken pieces in an 8x8x2-inch (20x20x5cm) baking dish. Pour brandy mixture over chicken. Turn pieces to coat.

Bake, covered, in a 350°F (180 °C) gas mark 4 oven for 30 to 35 minutes or until chicken is tender. Baste with cooking juices once. To serve, transfer chicken and cooking juices to a serving dish. Garnish with tarragon, if desired. Makes 4 servings.

Sensational Roasted Meats

Treat yourself to an elegant roast *and* stay trim. Not possible, you say? Yes, it is. Here's the proof. Choose lean cuts of meat, remove the excess fat, and watch calories disappear.

Roast Pork Florentine

Roast Pork Florentine

Ask your butcher to loosen the backbone—it makes the roast easier to carve.

  1 **3-pound (1kg350g) pork loin (centre cut), backbone loosened**
 10 **ounces (275g) frozen chopped spinach, thawed and well drained**
  2 **ounces (50g) grated carrot**
  1 **small apple, cored and chopped**
  ½ **teaspoon salt**
  ¼ **teaspoon dried basil, crushed**
  5½ **fluid ounces (155ml) tinned apple juice**
  1 **tablespoon soy sauce**
  2 **teaspoons cornflour**
  1 **ounce (25g) grated carrot**
  2 **tablespoons thinly sliced spring onion**
     Cherry tomatoes (optional)
     Parsley sprigs (optional)

270 calories per serving

Trim separable fat from meat (see photo 1, page 24). Cut eight pockets in the meaty side of roast (see photo 1). In a medium bowl stir together well-drained spinach, 2 ounces (50g) carrot, apple, salt, and basil. Spoon a generous 3 ounces (75g) of spinach mixture into each pocket (see photo 2).

Place roast, bone side down, in a shallow roasting tin. Insert a meat thermometer into the pork loin (see photo 3). Roast meat in a 325°F (170°C) gas mark 3 oven for 1¾ to 2¼ hours or till thermometer registers 170°F (80°C). Remove loin from the oven. Let stand 15 minutes to cool slightly.

For sauce, in a small saucepan combine apple juice, soy sauce, and cornflour. Stir in 1 ounce (25g) carrot and onion. Cook and stir till thickened and bubbly, then cook and stir 2 minutes more. Transfer loin to a cutting board. Cut away backbone, removing as little meat as possible (see photo 4). Place loin on a dish. Garnish with tomatoes and parsley, if desired. To serve, place a fork in top of loin to steady meat and cut between pockets. Serve sauce with meat. Makes 8 servings.

1 With a sharp knife, cut eight pockets in the meaty side of the pork loin. Position the pockets between the bones, as shown. The pockets should be cut about halfway into the meat of the pork loin.

3 Insert a meat thermometer into the end of the loin so its bulb rests in the centre of the thickest part of the meat. It should not rest in the filling or fat, or touch the bone or bottom of the pan. This ensures that the thermometer accurately measures the internal temperature of the meat.

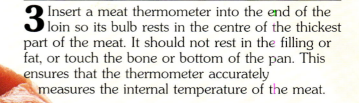

2 Hold the pocket open with one hand and spoon the spinach mixture into the pocket with the other hand, as shown. Notice the shape of the bone in the loin—it makes its own rack. When the rib bones are left on the loin, no rack is needed.

4 To make carving easier, remove the backbone after the loin is cooked. Begin by cutting between the meat and the bone, staying as close to the bone as possible. Then, gently pull the bone away from the meat as you continue cutting, removing as little of the meat as possible.

Roast Round of Beef with Vegetables

Chutney lends a delicate flavour to the meat and gives the roast a moist, glazed appearance.

1 **2-pound (900g) round roast**
Salt
Pepper
3 **tablespoons finely chopped chutney**
16 **ounces (450g) frozen French beans**
1 **large onion, cut into wedges**
4 **fluid ounces (110ml) apple juice**
2 **tablespoons chopped pimento**
1½ **teaspoons cornflour**
⅛ **teaspoon dried thyme, crushed**

169 calories per serving

Trim separable fat from meat (see photo 1, page 24). Place meat on a rack in a shallow roasting tin. Sprinkle with salt and pepper. Insert a meat thermometer into the roast (see photo 3, page 73). Roast in a 325°F (170°C) gas mark 3 oven for 1½ to 2 hours for rare or till thermometer registers 140°F (60°C). Roast to 160°F (70°C) for medium or to 170°F (80°C) for well-done. Spoon chutney over top of roast, then roast 10 to 15 minutes more. Remove meat from the oven. Let stand 15 minutes.

Meanwhile, for vegetables, in a covered saucepan cook French beans and onion in a small amount of boiling salted water for 4 to 5 minutes or till onion is tender. Drain beans and onions, then set aside. In the same saucepan combine apple juice, pimento, cornflour, and thyme. Cook and stir till thickened and bubbly, then cook and stir 2 minutes more. Stir in beans and onion. Carve meat into 16 thin slices. Serve on a dish with vegetables. Makes 8 servings.

Pork with Curry Relish

1 **2-pound (700-900g) boneless pork loin**
Salt
Pepper
4 **fluid ounces (110ml) cold water**
2 **teaspoons cornflour**
½ **to 1 teaspoon curry powder**
½ **teaspoon instant chicken bouillon granules**
1 **medium cooking apple, cored and chopped**
2 **tablespoons finely snipped dried apricots**

175 calories per serving

Trim separable fat from meat (see photo 1, page 24). Place meat on a rack in a shallow roasting tin. Sprinkle with salt and pepper. Insert a meat thermometer into the roast (see photo 3, page 73). Roast in a 325°F (170°C) gas mark 3 oven for 1 to 1¼ hours or till meat thermometer registers 170°F (80°C). Remove meat from the oven. Let meat stand 15 minutes.

Meanwhile, for sauce, in a medium saucepan combine water, cornflour, curry, and bouillon granules. Cook and stir till thickened and bubbly. Stir in apple and apricots. Cover and simmer for 2 to 3 minutes or till apple is tender, stirring occasionally. Carve meat into eight slices. Serve sauce over meat. Makes 8 servings.

Joint of Beef with Mushroom Sauce

A delicate wine flavour rounds out this mushroom sauce, so no one will suspect you're counting calories.

1	3-pound (1kg350g) joint of beef
½	teaspoon salt
½	teaspoon dried marjoram, crushed
¼	teaspoon pepper
14	fluid ounces (385ml) tinned beef broth
4	teaspoons cornflour
4	ounces (110g) tinned sliced mushrooms, drained
2	fluid ounces (55ml) dry red wine
⅛	teaspoon dried marjoram, crushed

163 calories per serving

Trim separable fat from meat (see photo 1, page 24). Place meat on a rack in a shallow roasting tin. In a small bowl combine salt, ½ teaspoon marjoram, and pepper, then rub over meat. Insert a meat thermometer into the roast (see photo 3, page 73). Roast in a 325°F (170°C) gas mark 3 oven for 1½ to 2 hours for medium-rare or until meat thermometer registers 150°F (65°C). Roast to 160°F (70°C) for medium or to 170°F (80°C) for well-done. Remove meat from oven. Let stand 15 minutes.

Meanwhile, for sauce, in a small saucepan combine beef broth and cornflour. Cook and stir till thickened and bubbly, then cook and stir 2 minutes more. Stir in mushrooms, red wine, and ⅛ teaspoon marjoram. Heat through. Carve roast by slicing across the grain into 10 slices. Serve sauce with meat. Makes 10 servings.

Veal à l'Orange

Cardamom, a distinctive spice belonging to the ginger family, subtly flavours the orange sauce.

1	3-pound (1kg350g) veal leg sirloin roast
8	fluid ounces (220ml) orange juice
1	tablespoon cornflour
¼	teaspoon chicken bouillon granules
¼	teaspoon ground cardamom
10	ounces (275g) tinned mandarin orange sections, drained
1	tablespoon orange liqueur (optional)

182 calories per serving

Trim separable fat from meat (see photo 1, page 24). Place meat on a rack in a shallow roasting tin. Insert a meat thermometer into the roast (see photo 3, page 73). Roast in a 325°F (170°C) gas mark 3 oven for 1¾ to 2 hours or until thermometer registers 170°F (80°C). Remove meat from the oven. Let stand 15 minutes before serving.

Meanwhile, for orange sauce, in a small saucepan combine orange juice, cornflour, bouillon granules, and cardamom. Cook and stir till thickened and bubbly, then cook and stir 2 minutes more. Add orange sections and orange liqueur, if desired. Heat through. Carve meat into 10 slices. Serve with orange sauce. Serves 10.

Spirited Marinades

Make your main dishes say delectable, not diet, with marinades. By soaking meats in flavoursome mixtures of herbs, spices, and wine or vinegar, you can give them lots of flavour with few calories. What's more, you can often recycle the marinade as a sauce.

Sherry-Marinated Steaks

Sherry-Marinated Steaks

**1 pound (450g) chuck *or* blade bone steak,
    cut ¾ inch (2cm) thick**
2 spring onions, sliced
1 clove garlic, minced
¼ teaspoon pepper
4 fluid ounces (110ml) dry sherry
**2½ ounces (60g) tinned sliced mushrooms,
    drained**
**1 tablespoon snipped parsley
    (see photo 4)**
2 teaspoons cornflour
**¼ teaspoon instant beef bouillon
    granules**
Spring onions (optional)
Tomato wedges (optional)

164 calories per serving

Trim separable fat from meat (see photo 1, page 24). Cut into four pieces and place in a polythene bag (see photo 1). Set bag in a deep bowl. Add sliced onion, garlic, and ¼ teaspoon *pepper*, then pour sherry over mixture (see photo 2). Close bag tightly and turn to coat meat. Marinate in the refrigerator for 8 to 24 hours, turning bag once or twice (see photo 3).

Drain steaks well, reserving marinade. Place on an unheated rack in a grill pan. Grill 3 inches from the heat for 5 minutes (see photo 2, page 48). Turn steaks with tongs and grill 5 to 6 minutes more or until cooked to suit.

Meanwhile, for sauce, add enough water to reserved marinade to measure 8 fluid ounces (220ml). In a small saucepan combine marinade mixture, mushrooms, parsley, cornflour, and bouillon granules. Cook and stir until thickened and bubbly, then cook and stir 2 minutes more. Place steaks on a hot dish (see photo 5). Spoon sauce over steaks. Garnish with whole spring onions and tomato wedges, if desired. Makes 4 servings.

1 Place the meat in a large polythene bag. Putting everything into one bag makes it easier to distribute the marinade and simplifies cleanup.

2 Pour the marinade mixture into the polythene bag, as shown. Place the polythene bag inside a deep bowl to prevent any accidental leakage and to make transporting the bag easier. Close the bag securely and turn it over a few times to coat all of the meat with the marinade mixture.

3 Remember to turn the polythene bag over occasionally during the marinating time, so that the marinade is evenly distributed over all the surfaces of the meat for more flavour.

4 Place a couple of sprigs of fresh parsley in a custard cup. Snip with kitchen shears. One or two sprigs will yield about 1 tablespoon of snipped parsley.

5 Keep the marinated steaks hot and juicy by serving them on a heated sizzle dish.

Fancy Fish Fillets

1 **pound (450g) fresh *or* frozen sole *or* flounder fillets**
2 **fluid ounces (55ml) water**
2 **fluid ounces (55ml) dry white wine**
½ **teaspoon dried basil, crushed**
½ **teaspoon instant chicken bouillon granules**
Cooking oil
8 **ounces (225g) frozen brussels sprouts**
6 **ounces (175g) natural low-fat yogurt**
4 **teaspoons cornflour**
1 **tablespoon chopped pimento**

147 calories per serving

Thaw fish, if frozen. Separate into fillets. Place fish in a polythene bag (see photo 1, page 78). Set bag in a deep bowl. For marinade, in a small bowl combine water, wine, basil, and bouillon granules. Pour marinade over fish in bag (see photo 2, page 78). Close bag tightly and turn bag to coat fish. Marinate for 1 hour at room temperature or 6 hours in the refrigerator, turning bag once or twice (see photo 3, page 78).

Drain fillets well, reserving the marinade. Coat a 12x7½x2-inch (30x19x5cm) baking dish with cooking oil. Place fillets in baking dish. Bake, uncovered, in a 450°F (230°C) gas mark 8 oven till fish flakes easily with a fork (see photo 3, page 85). Allow 5 to 6 minutes for each ½-inch (1cm) thickness.

Meanwhile for sauce, in a medium saucepan cook brussels sprouts according to package directions. Drain well. When cool enough to handle, cut brussels sprouts in half. In the same saucepan combine yogurt and cornflour. Stir in reserved marinade and pimento. Cook and stir till thickened and bubbly, then cook and stir 2 minutes more. Stir in brussels sprouts and heat through. Transfer fish to a serving dish. Spoon sauce over the fish. Makes 4 servings.

Harvest Pork Chops

Apple rings, apple juice, and pork chops—delicious!

4 **pork chops, cut ½ inch (1cm) thick (about 1⅓ pounds [600g])**
4 **fluid ounces (110ml) apple juice *or* apple cider**
1 **tablespoon snipped chives**
1 **clove garlic, minced**
¼ **teaspoon dried basil, crushed**
¼ **teaspoon dried oregano, crushed**
Salt
Pepper
4 **thinly sliced apple rings**

182 calories per serving

Trim separable fat from chops (see photo 1, page 24). Place chops in a polythene bag (see photo 1, page 78). Set bag in a deep bowl. For marinade, in a small bowl combine apple juice, chives, garlic, basil, and oregano. Pour over meat in bag (see photo 2, page 78). Close bag tightly and turn bag to coat meat. Marinate in the refrigerator for 8 to 24 hours, turning bag once or twice (see photo 3, page 78).

Drain chops well and place on an unheated rack in a grill pan. Grill chops 3 to 4 inches (7.5 to 10cm) from the heat for 6 minutes (see photo 2, page 48). Turn chops and grill 6 minutes more. Sprinkle with salt and pepper. Place an apple ring on top of each chop. Grill 2 minutes more. Makes 4 servings.

Lemon-Marinated Steak

1 **pound (450g) chuck *or* blade bone steak, cut ¾ inch (2cm) thick**
½ **teaspoon finely grated lemon peel**
3 **tablespoons lemon juice**
3 **tablespoons water**
1 **tablespoon cooking oil**
1 **tablespoon sliced spring onion**
1 **teaspoon Worcestershire sauce**
½ **teaspoon instant beef bouillon granules**
⅛ **teaspoon pepper**
Snipped parsley (optional)

157 calories per serving

Trim separable fat from meat (see photo 1, page 24). Pierce all surfaces of meat with a fork. Place meat in a polythene bag (see photo 1, page 78). Set bag in a deep bowl.

For marinade, in a small bowl combine lemon peel, lemon juice, water, oil, onion, Worcestershire sauce, bouillon granules, and pepper. Pour over meat in bag (see photo 2, page 78). Close bag tightly and turn to coat meat. Marinate in the refrigerator for 8 to 24 hours, turning bag once or twice (see photo 3, page 78).

Drain meat well, reserving marinade. Place meat on a rack in an unheated grill pan. Grill meat 4 inches (10cm) from heat for 5 minutes (see photo 2, page 48). Brush meat with marinade and turn with tongs. Grill for 5 to 7 minutes more or until cooked to suit, brushing with marinade occasionally. Transfer meat to a serving dish and carve across the grain into thin slices. Garnish with parsley, if desired. Makes 4 servings.

Pineapple-Sauced Fish

1 **pound (450g) fresh *or* frozen haddock fillets**
4 **fluid ounces (110ml) unsweetened pineapple juice**
1 **teaspoon minced dried onion**
¼ **teaspoon salt**
⅛ **teaspoon dried mint, crushed**
Cooking oil
1 **teaspoon cornflour**
2 **tablespoons snipped parsley (see photo 4, page 79)**
Mint sprigs (optional)

112 calories per serving

Thaw fish, if frozen. Separate into fillets. Place fish in a polythene bag (see photo 1, page 78). Set bag in a deep bowl. For marinade, in a small bowl combine pineapple juice, onion, salt, and mint. Pour over fish in bag (see photo 2, page 78). Close bag tightly and turn bag to coat fish. Marinate for 1 hour at room temperature or 6 hours in the refrigerator, turning once or twice.

Drain fish well, reserving the marinade. Coat a 12x7x2-inch (30x18x5cm) baking dish with cooking oil. Place fish in baking dish. (If fillets vary in thickness, turn under any thin portions.) Bake, uncovered, in a 450°F (230°C) gas mark 8 oven until fish flakes easily with a fork (see photo 3, page 85). Allow 5 to 6 minutes for each ½-inch (1cm) thickness.

Meanwhile, for sauce, in a small saucepan combine reserved marinade and cornflour. Cook and stir until thickened and bubbly, then cook and stir 2 minutes more. Transfer fish to a serving dish and serve with sauce. Sprinkle with parsley. Garnish with mint, if desired. Makes 4 servings.

Delicious Steamed Fish

Try steam heat! It's perfect for cooking fish. Not only does steaming keep the fish moist, it also helps the fish retain its shape and delicate texture. Because steam heat relies on water rather than heavy fats or oil, it makes for great low-calorie eating—naturally.

Spicy Steamed Fish

Spicy Steamed Fish

For a quick reference to other delicious fish selections, see the tip box on page 87.

1 **pound (450g) fresh *or* frozen halibut steaks *or* other lean fish steaks *or* fillets**
5½ **fluid ounces (155ml) tinned tomato or vegetable juice with a few drops of Worcestershire sauce**
1 **medium tomato, peeled, seeded, and chopped**
2 **tablespoons chopped onion**
2 **tablespoons chopped green pepper**
1 **teaspoon lemon juice**
   Fresh dill (optional)

196 calories per serving

Thaw fish, if frozen. For sauce, in a small saucepan combine tomato juice or vegetable juice, tomato, onion, green pepper, and lemon juice. Bring to boiling; reduce heat. Simmer, uncovered, about 12 minutes or until sauce thickens and is reduced to 8 fluid ounces (220ml).

Meanwhile, place a wire rack in a 10-inch (25.5cm) frying pan with a tight-fitting lid. Add water until it almost reaches the rack (see photo 1). Bring water to boiling. Place fish on the rack (see photo 2). Cover the pan and steam 6 to 8 minutes for steaks, 4 to 6 minutes per ½ inch (1cm) of thickness for fillets, or until fish flakes easily with a fork (see photo 3).

Carefully transfer fish from the rack to a serving dish (see photo 4). Pour sauce over fish. Garnish with dill, if desired. Makes 4 servings.

1 Pour water into a 10-inch (25.5cm) frying pan till it almost reaches the rack, as shown. If there's not enough water in the pan, all of it may boil away, scorching the pan. If there's too much water, the fish boils rather than steams and some of the fish flavour is lost in the steaming liquid.

2 Bring the water in the frying pan to boiling, then carefully arrange the fish steaks or fillets on the rack with tongs or a spatula, as shown. Don't use your hands to arrange the fish because the heat from the steam may burn them.

Test for degree of cooking

3 Insert fork prongs into fish at a 45-degree angle. Then, twist the fork gently. If fish resists flaking and is still translucent, it's underdone.

The fish is done when it is opaque and flakes easily.

The fish is overdone if it looks dry or mealy and falls apart easily.

 **Underdone**

 **Done**

 **Overdone**

4 Slide the spatula completely underneath each fish steak or fillet. This helps to keep the fish from breaking apart as you lift it. If you run the spatula parallel to the rungs of the rack, as shown, it is easier to get under the piece of fish than trying to go across the rungs.

Now, carefully transfer each piece of fish to a serving dish.

Steamed Salmon with Horseradish Sauce

Just enough horseradish to add a tang.

2 small fresh *or* frozen salmon steaks
   (½ pound (225g))
4 ounces (110ml) skimmed milk
1 tablespoon snipped chives *or* spring
   onion tops
1½ teaspoons cornflour
⅛ teaspoon salt
2 teaspoons horseradish sauce
½ teaspoon lemon juice
   Alfalfa sprouts (optional)
   Lemon wedges (optional)

208 calories per serving

Thaw fish, if frozen. Place a wire rack in a 10-inch (25.5cm) frying pan with a tight-fitting lid. Add water until it almost reaches rack (*see* photo 1, page 84). Bring water to boiling. Place steaks on rack (*see* photo 2, page 84). Cover pan and steam 6 to 8 minutes or till fish flakes easily with a fork (*see* photo 3, page 85).

Meanwhile, for sauce, in a small saucepan combine milk, chives or onion tops, cornflour, and salt. Cook and stir till thickened and bubbly; cook and stir 2 minutes more. Remove from heat, then stir in horseradish and lemon juice. Carefully transfer fish to a serving dish (*see* photo 4, page 85). Pour sauce atop. Garnish with alfalfa sprouts and lemon wedges, if desired. Makes 2 servings.

Microwave Directions: (See tip box, page 62). Place fish in an 8x8x2-inch (20x20x5cm) non-metal baking dish. Cover with vented cling-film. In a countertop microwave oven on 100% power (HIGH) cook for 3½ to 4 minutes or till fish flakes easily with a fork (*see* photo 3, page 85). In a small non-metal bowl combine milk, chives, cornflour, and salt. Micro-cook, uncovered, on 100% power (HIGH) for 1½ to 2½ minutes or till thickened and bubbly, stirring every 30 seconds. Stir in horseradish and lemon juice. Continue as above.

Steamed Snapper And Squash

½ pound (225g) fresh *or* frozen red
   snapper fillets *or* other lean fish
   fillets (2 fillets)
4 ounces (110g) courgette or yellow
   summer squash
3 ounces (75g) fresh *or* frozen
   mange tout
4 fluid ounces (110ml) cold water
1½ teaspoons cornflour
¾ teaspoon instant chicken bouillon
   granules
¼ teaspoon dried thyme, crushed
1 tablespoon butter *or* margarine
3 ounces (75g) hot cooked rice

250 calories per serving

Thaw fish, if frozen. Remove and discard skin, if present. Slice squash diagonally into ¼-inch-thick (½cm) pieces. Clean fresh mange tout and remove strings, if necessary (*see* photo 4, page 37). (*Or,* run warm water over frozen mange tout to thaw.)

Place a wire rack in a 10-inch (25.5cm) frying pan with a tight-fitting lid. Add water until it almost reaches the rack (*see* photo 1, page 84). Bring to boiling. Place fish, sliced squash, and mange tout on rack (*see* photo 2, page 84). Cover pan and steam for 4 to 6 minutes per ½-inch (1cm) thickness of fillets or till fish flakes easily with a fork and vegetables are crisp-tender (*see* photo 3, page 85).

Meanwhile, for sauce, in a small saucepan combine cold water, cornflour, bouillon granules, and thyme. Cook and stir till thickened and bubbly, then cook and stir 2 minutes more. Stir in the butter or margarine till melted.

Carefully transfer fish and vegetables from the rack to a serving dish (*see* photo 4, page 85). Serve sauce over fish, vegetables, and hot cooked rice. Makes 2 servings.

Vegetable-Sauced Fish Fillets

1 pound (450g) frozen fish fillets
1 medium carrot, cut into thin slices
1 stalk celery, cut into thin slices
8 fluid ounces (220ml) skimmed milk
1 tablespoon cornflour
¼ teaspoon salt
¼ teaspoon dried dill

201 calories per serving

Thaw fish at room temperature for 20 to 30 minutes. Cut into four portions. Place a rack in a 10-inch (25.5cm) frying pan with a tight-fitting lid. Add water until it almost reaches rack (see photo 1, page 84). Bring water to boiling. Place fish on rack (see photo 2, page 84). Cover pan and steam 12 to 14 minutes or until fish flakes easily with a fork (see photo 3, page 85).

Meanwhile, for sauce, in a small saucepan cook carrot and celery in a small amount of boiling salted water about 5 minutes or until crisp-tender; drain. In the same saucepan combine milk, cornflour, salt, and dill. Cook and stir until thickened and bubbly, then cook and stir 2 minutes more. Add vegetables and heat through.

Carefully transfer fish from the rack to a serving dish (see photo 4, page 85). Serve sauce over fish. Makes 4 servings.

Crab with Lime Sauce

2 pounds (900g) frozen cooked king crab legs
4 fluid ounces (110ml) cold water
¾ teaspoon instant chicken bouillon granules
½ teaspoon cornflour
2 tablespoons butter *or* margarine
5 teaspoons lime juice

195 calories per serving

Thaw crab. Cut into four pieces. Place a wire rack in a 10-inch (25.5cm) frying pan with a tight-fitting lid. Add water until it almost reaches rack (see photo 1, page 84). Bring water to boiling. Place crab on rack over boiling water (see photo 2, page 84). Cover and steam for 5 minutes or until hot.

For sauce, in a small saucepan combine cold water, bouillon granules, and cornflour. Cook and stir until thickened and bubbly, then cook and stir 2 minutes more. Add butter or margarine and lime juice. Stir until butter or margarine is melted. Use as a dip for crab. Serves 4.

Figuring Out Fish

All fish are not created equal! Although most fish are leaner than many types of meat and poultry, some fish are leaner than others. The leanest fish (with less than 5 percent fat) include cod, perch, flounder, sole, haddock, smelt, whiting, and red snapper. "Fat" fish include lake trout, eel, mackerel, tuna, salmon, swordfish, and whitefish. If you must severely limit your fat intake, depend on the first group. If not, both are deliciously low-calorie.

Sizzling Stir-Frys

Stir up excitement at meal time. Try your hand at stir-frying. As the name implies, this cooking method uses a constant stirring motion to quickly cook foods. That means you need very little fat or oil. The results are low-calorie and delicious.

Garlic Chicken

Garlic Chicken

2 **whole large chicken breasts (2 pounds [900g] total), skinned and boned (see photo 1, page 66)**
9 **ounces (250g) fresh mange tout *or* two 6-ounce packages frozen mange tout**
3 **large carrots**
4 **spring onions**
5 **cloves garlic**
3 **fluid ounces (75g) cold water**
3 **tablespoons soy sauce**
2 **tablespoons dry sherry**
1 **tablespoon cornflour**
2 **tablespoons cooking oil**

300 calories per serving

Cut chicken into 1-inch (2.5cm) pieces. Clean fresh mange tout and remove strings, if necessary (see photo 4, page 37). Or, run warm water over the frozen mange tout to thaw. Slice carrots and thinly slice onions (see photo 1). Mince garlic (see photos 2–3). Set aside.

In a small bowl combine cold water, soy sauce, sherry, and cornflour. Set aside.

Preheat a wok or large frying pan over high heat; add *half* of the cooking oil. Add carrots and garlic. Using a spatula or long-handled spoon, gently lift and turn the food with a folding motion. Keep food moving at all times or it will burn (see photo 4). Stir-fry for 3 minutes. Add mange tout and onions. Stir-fry for 2 minutes more or until vegetables are crisp-tender. Transfer vegetables to a bowl.

Add remaining cooking oil to the hot wok or frying pan. Add half of the chicken, then stir-fry about 3 minutes (see photo 5). Remove chicken. Stir-fry remaining chicken about 3 minutes. Return all chicken to the wok or frying pan. Push chicken from the centre of the wok. Stir cornflour mixture and add to the centre of the wok or frying pan. Cook and stir until thickened and bubbly, then cook and stir 1 minute more (see photo 6). Stir in vegetables and cover. Cook 1 minute more. Makes 5 servings.

1 Slice carrots by holding a sharp knife at a 45-degree angle to the cutting board. Cut each carrot into thin slices (about ⅛ inch [3mm] thick), as shown. These thin slices will cook quickly in the wok as well as give an attractive appearance to the finished dish. The spring onions, along with some of their green tops, are cut into thin slices, as shown at the top of the cutting board.

2 Working on a cutting board, crush garlic by holding a wide-blade knife over a clove. Lightly pound the knife with your fist, moving the knife forward to loosen the peel. If you own a garlic press, you'll find it a handy way to mince garlic, too.

3 Remove the thin peel from the garlic and discard it. Cut the garlic into very tiny pieces with a sharp knife, as shown.

4 Use a wide spatula or long-handled spoon to stir-fry. Gently lift and turn the food with a folding motion. Keep the food moving so that it cooks evenly without burning.

6 Push the chicken from the centre of the wok. Stir the corn-flour mixture and pour it into the centre of the wok. Cook and stir the mixture until thickened and bubbly, as shown.

5 Stir-fry the chicken with the same fold-ing motion, making sure all sides are cooked. You'll know when the chicken is done by the change in color from pink to beige.

Pork and Courgette Stir-Fry

1   **pound (450g) lean boneless pork**
2   **carrots, thinly sliced (see photo 1, page 90)**
2   **fluid ounces (55ml) cold water**
2   **tablespoons soy sauce**
1   **tablespoon cornflour**
1   **teaspoon sugar**
½   **teaspoon instant chicken bouillon granules**
2   **small courgettes, cut into julienne strips**
2   **tablespoons cooking oil**
3   **ounces (75g) sliced fresh mushrooms**

234 calories per serving

Trim separable fat from meat (see photo 1, page 24). Partially freeze meat. With a sharp knife thinly slice meat across the grain into bite-size strips (see photo 1, page 60). In a medium saucepan cook carrots in boiling water for 2 to 3 minutes or until crisp-tender; drain. In a small bowl stir together cold water, soy sauce, cornflour, sugar, and bouillon granules. Set aside.

Coat a wok or frying pan with *1 tablespoon* cooking oil. Preheat the wok or frying pan over high heat. *(See stir-frying photos 4–6, page 91.)* Add courgettes and stir-fry for 2 to 3 minutes or until crisp-tender; remove from wok or pan. Add *1 tablespoon* cooking oil to the wok or frying pan. Add *half* of meat. Stir-fry for 2 to 3 minutes or until no longer pink. Remove meat from wok or frying pan. Stir-fry remaining pork for 2 to 3 minutes or until no longer pink. Return all of the meat to the wok or frying pan. Push meat from centre of the wok or pan. Stir cornflour mixture, then add to centre of wok or frying pan. Cook and stir until thickened and bubbly. Stir in carrots, courgettes, and mushrooms and cover. Cook 1 to 2 minutes more. Makes 4 servings.

Orange-Beef Stir-Fry

¾   **pound (350g) chuck *or* blade bone steak**
1½   **pounds (700g) broccoli, cut into 1-inch (2.5cm) pieces**
½   **teaspoon finely grated orange peel**
4   **fluid ounces (110ml) orange juice**
2   **tablespoons soy sauce**
2   **teaspoons cornflour**
2   **medium oranges**
    Cooking oil

183 calories per serving

Trim separable fat from meat (see photo 1, page 24). Partially freeze meat. With a sharp knife thinly slice meat across the grain into bite-size strips (see photo 1, page 60). In a medium saucepan cook broccoli, covered, in a small amount of boiling water about 5 minutes or until crisp-tender; drain. Set aside. In a small bowl stir together orange peel, orange juice, soy sauce, and cornflour. Set aside.

Working over a bowl, peel and section oranges. First, cut off the peel and white membrane. Then, remove the sections by cutting into the centre of the fruit between one section and the membrane. Turn the knife and slide it down the other side of the section next to the membrane. Remove any seeds.

Coat the wok or large frying pan with cooking oil. Preheat the wok or frying pan over high heat. *(See stir-frying photos 4–6, page 91.)* Using a long-handled utensil stir-fry meat for 2 to 3 minutes or until brown. Push meat from centre of wok or frying pan. Stir cornflour mixture, then add to centre of wok or frying pan. Cook and stir until thickened and bubbly. Stir in broccoli and orange sections and cover. Cook 1 minute more. Makes 4 servings.

Sesame Veal

1 pound (450g) boneless veal *or* lean pork
4 fluid ounces (110ml) water
2 tablespoons sake *or* dry sherry
1 tablespoon cornflour
1 teaspoon instant chicken bouillon granules
¼ teaspoon ground ginger *or* ½ teaspoon grated root ginger
2 tablespoons cooking oil
16 ounces (450g) fresh asparagus, cut into 1-inch (2.5cm) pieces, *or* 9 ounces (250g) frozen cut asparagus, thawed
4 spring onions, sliced into ¼-inch (½cm) pieces
2 medium tomatoes, seeded and cut into thin wedges
1 tablespoon sesame seeds, toasted

289 calories per serving

Trim separable fat from meat (see photo 1, page 24). Partially freeze meat. With a sharp knife thinly slice meat across the grain into bite-size strips (see photo 1, page 60). In a bowl combine water, sake or sherry, cornflour, bouillon granules, and ginger. Set aside.

Preheat a wok or large frying pan over high heat; add *half* of the cooking oil. *(See stir-frying photos 4–6, page 91.)* Stir-fry asparagus and onions for 1 minute. Remove from the wok.

Add remaining oil to the wok or frying pan. Add *half* of the veal or pork, then stir-fry for 2 minutes. Remove meat. Stir-fry remaining meat for 2 minutes. Return all meat to wok or frying pan. Push meat from the centre of the wok or frying pan. Stir cornflour mixture, then add to the centre of the wok or pan. Cook and stir till thickened and bubbly. Return vegetables to wok or frying pan. Cook and stir 1 minute. Add tomato wedges and cover. Cook 1 minute more. Sprinkle with sesame seeds. Makes 4 servings.

Prawn and Spinach Stir-Fry

Thaw frozen prawns by running cold water over them.

12 ounces (350g) fresh *or* frozen prawns in shells
4 fluid ounces (110ml) unsweetened pineapple juice
2 teaspoons cornflour
2 tablespoons cooking oil
12 ounces (350g) torn fresh spinach
12 cherry tomatoes, halved

174 calories per serving

Thaw prawns, if frozen. Shell and devein prawns (see tip box, below). Halve prawns lengthwise. In a bowl stir together pineapple juice, cornflour, and dash *pepper*. Set aside.

Preheat a wok or frying pan over high heat; add oil. *(See stir-frying photos 4–6, page 91.)* Stir-fry prawns for 2 to 3 minutes. Push prawns from the centre of wok or frying pan. Stir cornflour mixture, then add to centre of the wok. Cook and stir till thickened and bubbly, then cook and stir 1 minute more. Stir in spinach and tomatoes and cover. Cook 1 minute more. Serves 4.

Shelling Prawns

To shell prawns, peel off the legs. Then, hold each prawn in one hand and peel back the shell with the other hand. Now, cut the body portion of the shell off, leaving the tail shell in place. Or, gently pull on the tail and remove the tail and shell. Leave the tail on when you're making prawn cocktail or any food eaten by hand. Finally, make a slit along the back of each prawn and use the tip of a knife to scrape out the black vein. Rinse the prawns.

Outstanding Omelettes

An egg is an egg is an egg—except when it's an omelette! Turn this traditional breakfast favourite into a low-calorie anytime meal. Our fluffy, delicate omelettes are stuffed with an assortment of calorie-trimmed fillings and are cooked with the barest minimum of cooking oil. Turn the pages and find exquisite omelettes, sure to satisfy even the most discriminating palate.

Asparagus-Cheese Omelette

Asparagus-Cheese Omelettes

In season, use ½ pound (225g) fresh asparagus in place of the frozen, but pre-cook it for 10 to 15 minutes.

10 ounces (275g) frozen asparagus *or* broccoli spears
3 ounces (75g) sliced fresh mushrooms
6 fluid ounces (165ml) skimmed milk
2 teaspoons cornflour
2 tablespoons grated cheddar cheese *or* crumbled blue cheese
8 eggs
2 fluid ounces (55ml) water
½ teaspoon salt
⅛ teaspoon pepper
Cooking oil
Snipped parsley (optional)

235 calories per serving

For filling, in a medium saucepan cook asparagus or broccoli spears and mushrooms in 4 fluid ounces (110ml) boiling salted water for 5 minutes or until crisp-tender. Drain well, then keep warm.

For sauce, in a small saucepan combine milk, cornflour, and dash *salt*. Cook and stir until thickened and bubbly, then cook and stir 2 minutes more. Stir in cheddar or blue cheese until it is melted. Keep warm over low heat.

To make omelettes, in a bowl beat together eggs, water, ½ teaspoon salt, and pepper until combined but not frothy (see photo 1). Coat a 6- or 8-inch (15 or 20cm) frying pan with cooking oil, then heat the pan. Add *one-fourth* of the egg mixture, about 4 fluid ounces (110ml) (see photo 2). Cook eggs over medium heat. As eggs set, run a spatula around edge of the pan, lifting eggs to allow uncooked portion to flow underneath (see photo 3). When eggs are set but still shiny, remove from the heat. Fill omelette with *one-fourth* of the filling and transfer to a warm serving plate (see photos 4–5). Cover with foil to keep warm.

To make *each* of the three remaining omelettes, add *½ teaspoon* oil to the hot frying pan. Spread oil evenly by tilting and rotating the pan. Cook and fill as above. Serve sauce with omelettes. Sprinkle with parsley, if desired. Makes 4 servings.

1 Beat together the eggs, water, salt, and pepper with a wire whisk or fork until they're combined but not frothy. Overbeating incorporates too much air into the eggs and gives you a rubbery omelette.

2 Start by pouring *one-fourth* of the egg mixture into the heated frying pan, as shown. Using a pan with flared sides makes it easier to remove the omelette, but a straight-sided pan will work.

3 As the eggs set, run a spatula around the edge of the frying pan, lifting the cooked eggs to allow the uncooked portion to flow underneath, as shown. Tipping the pan slightly helps.

Do not let the frying pan become too hot or the eggs will be overcooked and tough. Medium heat works best.

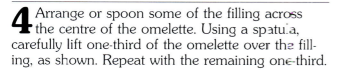

4 Arrange or spoon some of the filling across the centre of the omelette. Using a spatula, carefully lift one-third of the omelette over the filling, as shown. Repeat with the remaining one-third.

5 Slide the omelette to the side of the frying pan. Tilt the pan and slide the omelette out onto a warm plate, as shown. Cover with foil to keep the omelette warm while preparing the other omelettes.

Southwestern Omelettes

1 medium tomato, peeled, seeded, and chopped
2½ ounces (60g) green chilli peppers, rinsed, seeded, and chopped
2 tablespoons sliced spring onion
1 tablespoon snipped parsley
1 small clove garlic, minced
   Dash salt
   Dash ground red pepper
4 eggs
2 tablespoons water
¼ teaspoon salt
   Dash pepper
   Cooking oil
1 ounce (25g) grated Gouda *or* Monterey Jack cheese *or* Monterey Jack cheese with jalapeño peppers

259 calories per serving

For filling, in a small saucepan mix tomato, chilli peppers, onion, parsley, garlic, dash salt, and red pepper. Simmer about 3 minutes or till heated through; stir often. Keep warm.

(See omelette-making photos 1–5, pages 96–97.) To make omelettes, in a bowl beat together eggs, water, ¼ teaspoon salt, and pepper till combined but not frothy. Coat a 6- or 8-inch (15 or 20cm) frying pan with cooking oil, then heat the pan. Add *one-half* of the egg mixture, about 4 fluid ounces (110ml), then cook over medium heat. As eggs set, run a spatula around edge of the frying pan, lifting the eggs to allow uncooked portion to flow underneath. When eggs are set but still shiny, remove from the heat. Fill each omelette with *one-half* of the filling and transfer to a warm serving plate. Cover with foil to keep warm while the others cook.

To make remaining omelette, add ½ *teaspoon* cooking oil to the hot frying pan. Spread oil evenly by tilting and rotating the frying pan. Cook and fill as above. Sprinkle cheese over omelettes. Makes 2 servings.

Chicken and Artichoke Omelettes

8 fluid ounces (220ml) skimmed milk
1 tablespoon cornflour
1 tablespoon French mustard
¼ teaspoon dried tarragon, crushed
9 ounces (250g) frozen artichoke hearts, cooked, drained, and cut up
5 ounces (150g) diced cooked chicken
6 eggs
3 tablespoons water
½ teaspoon salt
⅛ teaspoon pepper
   Cooking oil

248 calories per serving

For filling, in a saucepan combine skimmed milk and cornflour. Cook and stir till thickened and bubbly, then cook and stir for 2 minutes more. Stir in mustard and tarragon. Stir in artichokes and chicken, then heat through. Keep warm.

(See omelette-making photos 1–5, pages 96–97.) To make omelettes, in a bowl beat together eggs, water, salt, and pepper till combined but not frothy. Coat a 6- or 8-inch (15 or 20cm) frying pan with cooking oil, then heat the frying pan. Add *one-fourth* of the egg mixture, about 3 fluid ounces (80ml), then cook over medium heat. As eggs set, run a spatula around the edge of the pan, lifting the eggs to allow uncooked portion to flow underneath. When eggs are set but still shiny, remove from the heat. Fill omelette with *one-fourth* of the filling and transfer to a warm serving dish. Cover with foil to keep warm.

To make *each* of the three remaining omelettes, add ½ *teaspoon* cooking oil to the hot frying pan. Spread oil evenly by tilting and rotating the pan. Cook and fill as above. Makes 4 servings.

Pizza Omelettes

14½ ounces (410g) tinned peeled Italian-style tomatoes, cut up
1 tablespoon dried parsley flakes
½ teaspoon caster sugar
½ teaspoon dried basil, crushed
½ teaspoon dried oregano, crushed
2 ounces (50g) sliced pepperoni, halved
6 eggs
3 tablespoons water
½ teaspoon minced dried onion
½ teaspoon dried parsley flakes
¼ teaspoon garlic salt
   Dash pepper
   Cooking oil
1 ounce (25g) grated Parmesan cheese

256 calories per serving

For filling, in a medium saucepan mix *un-drained* tomatoes, 1 tablespoon parsley flakes, sugar, basil, and oregano. Bring mixture to boiling. Add pepperoni. Reduce the heat and simmer, uncovered, for 10 to 12 minutes or until slightly thickened.

(See omelette-making photos 1–5, pages 96–97.) To make omelettes, in a bowl beat together eggs, water, onion, ½ teaspoon parsley flakes, garlic salt, and pepper until combined but not frothy. Coat a 6- or 8-inch (15 or 20cm) frying pan with cooking oil, then heat the frying pan. Add *one-fourth* of the egg mixture, about 3 fluid ounces (80ml), then cook over medium heat. As eggs set, run a spatula around edge of the frying pan, lifting the eggs to allow uncooked portion to flow underneath. When eggs are set but still shiny, remove from the heat. Reserve about *3 ounces (175g)* of the filling. Fill omelette with *one-fourth* of the remaining filling and transfer to a warm dish. Cover with foil to keep warm.

To make *each* of the three remaining omelettes, add ½ *teaspoon* cooking oil to the hot frying pan. Spread oil evenly by tilting and rotating the pan. Cook and fill as above. Top omelettes with reserved filling and cheese. Makes 4 servings.

Greek Omelettes

Feta cheese, pronounced (FEHT-ah), is white and crumbly with a salty flavour.

10 ounces (275g) frozen chopped spinach
8 eggs
2 fluid ounces (55ml) water
¼ teaspoon salt
¼ teaspoon ground nutmeg
⅛ teaspoon onion powder
⅛ teaspoon pepper
2 ounces (50g) crumbled feta cheese
   Cooking oil
2 ounces (50g) natural low-fat yogurt

241 calories per serving

For filling, in a medium saucepan cook spinach according to packet directions; drain in colander. Squeeze out the excess liquid by pressing the spinach against the colander with the back of a wooden spoon. Keep warm.

(See omelette-making photos 1–5, pages 96–97.) To make omelettes, in a bowl beat together eggs, water, salt, nutmeg, onion powder, and pepper until combined but not frothy. Coat a 6- or 8-inch (15 or 20cm) frying pan with cooking oil, then heat the pan. Add *one-fourth* of the egg mixture, about 4 fluid ounces (110ml), then cook over medium heat. As eggs set, run a spatula around edge of the frying pan, lifting the eggs to allow uncooked portion to flow underneath. When eggs are set but still shiny, remove from the heat. Spoon about *one-fourth* of the filling across the centre. Sprinkle with *one-fourth* of the feta cheese. Fold omelette and transfer to a warm serving dish. Cover with foil to keep warm.

To make *each* of the three remaining omelettes, add ½ *teaspoon* oil to the hot frying pan. Spread oil evenly by tilting and rotating the pan. Cook and fill as above. Dollop omelettes with yogurt. Makes 4 servings.

Classic Pancakes

Deliciously thin pancakes add flair to any meal. By trimming the cooking oil and reducing the number of eggs, we've created a pancake recipe that's a calorie-counter's delight. Fill regular or whole wheat pancakes with any one of five scrumptious fillings.

Cheesy Ham-Filled Pancakes

Calorie-Counter's Pancakes

12	fluid ounces (330ml) skimmed milk
5	ounces (150g) plain flour *or* whole wheat flour
1	egg
1	egg white
	Cooking oil

38 calories per pancake

In a bowl combine milk, flour, egg, and egg white. Beat with a rotary whisk until blended. Coat a 6-inch (15cm) frying pan with cooking oil. Place over medium heat until a drop of water sizzles (see photo 1). Remove from heat. Spoon in *2 tablespoons* batter. Tilt frying pan to spread batter (see photo 2). Return to heat, then brown on one side, about 1 minute. (*Or,* cook on an inverted pancake pan.) Run a metal spatula around edge of pancake to loosen. Invert frying pan and remove pancake (see photo 3). Lightly greasing pan occasionally, repeat to make 18 pancakes.

1 Heat the frying pan over medium heat. Sprinkle a few drops of water on the hot surface. If the water sizzles, as shown, the pan is ready to use.

When making the remaining pancakes, remember to grease lightly with cooking oil.

2 Pour *2 tablespoons* of the pancake batter into the heated frying pan. Lift and tilt the pan, as shown, so the batter covers the pan in a thin, even layer. If batter won't swirl to coat, thin it in the bowl with a little water and refill the frying pan. If there's a tear in the pancake or a bubble breaks leaving a hole, patch it with a little extra batter.

Cheesy Ham-Filled Pancakes

8	Calorie-Counter's Pancakes (see recipe, left)
10	ounces (275g) frozen chopped broccoli
8	fluid ounces (220ml) skimmed milk
1	tablespoon cornflour
2	ounces (50g) grated processed cheese
1	teaspoon prepared mustard
4	ounces (110g) fully cooked ham, finely chopped
2½	ounces (60g) tinned sliced mushrooms, drained
	Snipped chives

238 calories per serving

Prepare pancakes (see photos 1–3). Set aside. Cook broccoli according to packet directions. Drain and set aside. In saucepan mix milk and cornflour. Cook and stir until thickened and bubbly. Add cheese and mustard, then cook and stir until cheese is melted. Reserve 4 fluid ounces (110ml) of the sauce.

For filling, stir broccoli, ham, and mushrooms into remaining sauce, then heat through. Spoon about 3 fluid ounces (80ml) filling down the centre of each pancake, then fold the sides over (see photo 4). Arrange pancakes in a 12x7½x2-inch (30x19x5cm) baking dish. Pour reserved sauce over pancakes. Bake, covered, in a 350°F (180°C) gas mark 4 oven for 15 to 20 minutes. Sprinkle chives over pancakes. Serves 4.

3 Invert the pancake over kitchen paper, as shown. Let the pancake fall, then smooth it out, if necessary, so that the pancake lies flat.

4 Spoon the filling along the centre of the un-browned side of the pancake, as shown. Fold two sides of pancake to the centre so they overlap.

Stacked Prawn Creole

8   **Calorie-Counter's Pancakes (see recipe, page 102)**
¾   **pound (350g) fresh *or* frozen shelled prawns**
16   **ounces tinned tomatoes, cut up**
4   **ounces (110g) chopped onion**
4   **ounces (110g) chopped green pepper**
3   **ounces (75g) chopped celery**
1   **clove garlic, minced**
1   **bay leaf**
½   **teaspoon salt**
½   **teaspoon dried thyme, crushed**
⅛   **teaspoon ground red pepper**
4   **teaspoons cornflour**
2   **tablespoons snipped parsley**

216 calories per serving

Prepare pancakes (see photos 1–3, pages 102–103). Set aside. Thaw prawns, if frozen. In a 10-inch (25.5cm) frying pan combine *undrained* tomatoes, next eight ingredients, and 2 fluid ounces (55ml) *water*. Cover and simmer for 15 minutes or until celery is tender. Stir together cornflour and 2 tablespoons cold *water,* then add to tomato mixture. Cook and stir until thickened and bubbly. Stir in prawns and return to boiling. Cover and simmer for 5 minutes or until prawns are done. Remove bay leaf.

Place one pancake, brown side up, on a plate. Top with *2 ounces (50g)* prawn mixture, then another pancake and *2 ounces (50g)* prawn mixture. Repeat to make four stacks. Sprinkle with parsley. Makes 4 servings.

Freezing Pancakes

Keep extra pancakes on hand by freezing them. Stack pancakes alternately with two layers of greaseproof paper. Pack the stack in a moisture- and vapour-proof bag. Freeze for up to four months.

Sweet-Sour Pork Pancakes

8   **Calorie-Counter's Pancakes (see recipe, page 102)**
¾   **pound (350g) lean boneless pork Cooking oil**
4   **ounces (110g) chopped green pepper**
1   **clove garlic, minced**
2   **ounces (50g) finely grated carrot**
1½   **ounces (40g) caster sugar**
2   **fluid ounces (55ml) white wine vinegar**
1   **teaspoon instant beef bouillon granules**
1   **teaspoon soy sauce**
2   **tablespoons cornflour**
  Snipped parsley

267 calories per serving

Prepare pancakes (see photos 1–3, pages 102–103). Set aside. Trim separable fat from pork (see photo 1, page 24). Partially freeze pork. Thinly slice across grain into bite-size strips (see photo 1, page 60). Coat a 10-inch (25.5cm) frying pan with cooking oil, then heat. Add pork, green pepper, and garlic. Cook, stirring occasionally, until pork is no longer pink.

In a small saucepan mix carrot, sugar, vinegar, bouillon granules, soy sauce, and 8 fluid ounces (220ml) *water*, then bring to boiling. Combine 3 fluid ounces (80ml) cold *water* and cornflour. Add to carrot mixture. Cook and stir until thickened and bubbly, then cook and stir for 2 minutes more. Reserve about *4 ounces (110g)* sauce. Stir remaining sauce into pork mixture.

Spoon about *2 ounces (50g)* filling down the centre of each pancake, then fold sides over (see photo 4, page 103). Arrange pancakes in a 12x7½x2-inch (30x19x5cm) baking dish, then top with reserved sauce. Bake, covered, in a 350°F (180°C) gas mark 4 oven for 15 to 20 minutes or until heated through. Trim with parsley. Makes 4 servings.

Turkey Pancakes

Splurge with a dollop of cranberry sauce. It's well worth the few extra calories.

8 **Calorie-Counter's Pancakes (see recipe, page 102)**
1 **small apple, cored and chopped**
4 **ounces (110g) chopped celery**
2 **tablespoons chopped onion**
2 **tablespoons snipped parsley**
2 **tablespoons water**
½ **teaspoon salt**
¼ **teaspoon poultry seasoning**
⅛ **teaspoon pepper**
½ **pint (275ml) skimmed milk**
4 **teaspoons cornflour**
10 **ounces (275g) diced cooked turkey** *or* **chicken**
   Cranberry sauce (optional)

280 calories per serving

Prepare pancakes (see photos 1–3, pages 102–103). Set aside. In a small saucepan combine apple, celery, onion, parsley, water, salt, poultry seasoning, and pepper. Cook, covered for 5 to 6 minutes or until vegetables are tender. Drain. Stir together milk and cornflour, then add to the saucepan. Cook and stir until thickened and bubbly, then cook and stir for 2 minutes more. Reserve *4 fluid ounces (110ml)* of the sauce.

Stir turkey or chicken into remaining sauce and heat through. Spoon about 1½ ounces (40g) turkey mixture down the centre of each crepe, then fold sides over (see photo 4, page 103). Arrange the pancakes in a 12x7½x2-inch (30x19x5cm) baking dish. Pour the reserved sauce over pancakes. Bake, covered, in a 350°F (180°C) gas mark 4 oven for 15 to 20 minutes or until heated through. Dollop pancakes with cranberry sauce, if desired. Makes 4 servings.

Beef Stroganoff Cups

Pancake cups are a fun twist on the traditional roll-up.

4 **Calorie-Counter's Pancakes (see recipe, page 102)**
   Cooking oil
¾ **pound (350g) chuck *or* blade bone steak**
1 **tablespoon cooking oil**
3 **ounces (75g) sliced fresh mushrooms**
2 **ounces (50g) finely chopped onion**
4 **fluid ounces (110ml) beef broth**
4 **ounces (110g) soured cream**
1 **tablespoon plain flour**
   Parsley sprigs

220 calories per serving

Prepare pancakes (see photos 1–3, pages 102–103). Invert four custard cups on a baking tray, then coat with cooking oil. Place one pancake, brown side up, on top of each cup. Press pancake over cup, pinching to form three or four pleats. Bake in a 375°F (190°C) gas mark 5 oven for 20 minutes or until crisp. Remove from the oven and cool.

Trim separable fat from meat (see photo 1, page 24). Partially freeze meat. Thinly slice meat across the grain into bite-size strips (see photo 1, page 60). Preheat a wok or frying pan over high heat and add cooking oil. Stir-fry mushrooms and onion for 2 to 3 minutes. Transfer vegetables to a bowl. Stir-fry meat for 3 to 4 minutes (see photo 5, page 91). Push meat from centre of wok, then add beef broth to centre of wok. Stir together soured cream and flour and stir into beef broth. Cook and stir until thickened and bubbly, then cook and stir for 1 minute more. Return vegetables to wok. Cover and cook 1 minute. Spoon mixture into pancake cups. Garnish with parsley. Serves 4.

Satisfying Dinner Pies

A dieter's dream come true, these dinner pies feature a low-calorie pastry crust that substitutes cottage cheese for some of the fat in regular pastry. The result—a crisp crust with a whole wheat texture and appearance.

Terrific Taco Pie

Calorie-Trimmed Pastry

3 ounces (75g) low-fat cream-style
   cottage cheese
5 ounces (150g) plain flour
¼ teaspoon salt
3 tablespoons lard
2 to 3 tablespoons cold water

143 calories for ⅙ of pastry

Push cottage cheese through a sieve with a spoon (see photo 1). In a bowl stir together flour and salt. Cut in lard until pieces are the size of small peas (see photo 2). Add cottage cheese to flour mixture and combine with a fork. Sprinkle *1 tablespoon* cold water over part of the mixture. Toss with a fork. Push to the side of the bowl. Repeat with remaining water until all is moistened. Form into a ball (see photo 3).

On a lightly floured surface flatten dough with hands. Roll from centre to edge, forming a 12-inch (30cm) circle (see photo 4). Wrap around a rolling pin. Unroll into a 9-inch (23cm) pie plate (see photo 5). Ease pastry into pie plate (do not stretch). Trim to ½ inch (1cm) beyond edge of plate. Fold under extra pastry. Flute edge (see photo 6). Fill and bake as directed. Makes 1 (9-inch [23cm]) shell.

Terrific Taco Pie

Calorie-Trimmed Pastry
   (see recipe, left)
1 pound (450g) lean minced beef
4 ounces (110g) chopped onion
2 ounces (50g) chopped green pepper
1 clove garlic, minced
8 ounces (225g) tinned sieved tomatoes
½ to 1 teaspoon chilli powder
4 fluid ounces (110ml) taco sauce
1 tablespoon cornflour
2 ounces (50g) grated processed cheese
1½ ounces (40g) shredded lettuce
½ of a medium tomato, chopped

367 calories per serving

Prepare pastry shell and line with heavy foil (see photo 7). Bake in a 450°F (230°C) gas mark 8 oven about 15 minutes or until light brown. Carefully remove foil. Reduce the oven temperature to 350°F (180°C) gas mark 4. In a 10-inch (25.5cm) frying pan cook beef, onion, green pepper, and garlic until meat is brown. Drain off fat. Stir in sieved tomatoes and chilli powder. Stir together taco sauce and cornflour. Stir into frying pan; cook and stir until bubbly. Turn into pastry shell. Bake for 15 minutes. Sprinkle cheese over pie. Let stand for 5 minutes. Top with lettuce and tomato. Makes 6 servings.

1 Working over a mixing bowl, use the back of a wooden spoon to push the cottage cheese through a sieve, as shown.

2 Use a pastry blender to cut lard into the flour mixture until pieces are the size of small peas, as shown. Or, use two knives and cut through the mixture with a crossing motion.

The key to light, flaky pastry is to avoid blending the lard completely with the flour.

3 Moisten all of the flour mixture with water, then use a fork to form the dough into a ball, as shown. Use your hands to help shape the ball.

4 Flatten pastry with your hands and smooth the edges. Roll the dough with a rolling pin from the centre to the edges with light, even strokes, forming a 12-inch (30cm) circle.

5 Loosely unroll the pastry into a 9-inch (23cm) pie plate, as shown. Avoid stretching the pastry, or it will shrink as it bakes.

6 Flute the edge of the pastry by pressing the dough between two index fingers, as shown, or with the forefinger of one hand against the thumb and forefinger of the other hand. This gives a decorative edge and helps reduce shrinkage.

7 Line the pastry shell with a double thickness of heavy-duty foil, pressing down firmly but carefully. The foil keeps the pastry from puffing up or shrinking during baking.

Pork Pot Pie

It's your choice—leftover pork, chicken, beef, turkey, and ham work equally well in this savoury pie.

Calorie-Trimmed Pastry (see recipe, page 108)
10 **ounces (275g) frozen peas and carrots**
8 **fluid ounces (220ml) water**
3 **ounces (75g) chopped celery**
4 **ounces (110g) chopped onion**
1 **ounce (25g) snipped parsley**
3 **tablespoons cornflour**
2 **teaspoons instant chicken bouillon granules**
¼ **teaspoon salt**
¼ **teaspoon ground sage**
¼ **teaspoon dried thyme, crushed**
⅛ **teaspoon pepper**
8 **fluid ounces (220ml) skimmed milk**
10 **ounces (275g) cubed cooked pork**

321 calories per serving

Prepare pastry, *except* roll into a 12x8-inch (30x20cm) rectangle (see photos 1–4, pages 108–109). Set aside. In a large saucepan cook peas and carrots, water, celery, onion, and parsley for 5 to 8 minutes or until celery is tender. In a bowl stir together cornflour, bouillon granules, salt, sage, thyme, and pepper, then stir in milk. Stir into vegetable mixture. Cook and stir until thickened and bubbly. Stir in pork and heat through.

Turn the hot mixture into a 10x6x2-inch (25.5x15x5cm) baking dish. Place pastry over filling. Crimp pastry against edge of dish. Cut slits for escape of steam. Bake in a 425°F (220°C) gas mark 7 oven for 25 to 30 minutes or until top is light brown. Let stand for 10 minutes before serving. Makes 6 servings.

Chicken-Chilli Pepper Quiche

Calorie-Trimmed Pastry (see recipe, page 108)
3 **slightly beaten eggs**
½ **pint (275ml) semi-skimmed milk**
4 **ounces (110g) grated Edam *or* Gouda cheese**
4 **ounces (110g) chopped cooked chicken *or* turkey**
4 **ounces (110g) tinned diced green chilli peppers, rinsed and drained**
½ **teaspoon salt**
⅛ **teaspoon pepper**
Several dashes bottled hot pepper sauce
1 **medium tomato, sliced**
Parsley sprigs (optional)

334 calories per serving

Prepare pastry shell (see photos 1–6, pages 108–109). Line pastry shell with heavy foil (see photo 7, page 109). Bake in a 450°F (230°C) gas mark 8 oven about 15 minutes or till light brown. Carefully remove foil. Reduce the oven temperature to 325°F (170°C) gas mark 3.

Meanwhile, in a large bowl combine eggs, milk, cheese, chicken or turkey, chilli peppers, salt, pepper, and hot pepper sauce. Pour into baked pastry shell.

Bake in the 325°F (170°C) gas mark 3 oven for 35 to 40 minutes or till a knife inserted near the centre comes out clean. Remove from the oven, then top with tomato slices. Let stand for 10 minutes before serving. Garnish with parsley sprigs, if desired. Makes 6 servings.

Ham and Cheese Quiche

When we say cheese, we mean cheese! This delicate quiche has cottage cheese in the crust and two kinds of cheese in the filling.

Calorie-Trimmed Pastry (see recipe, page 108)
8 ounces (225g) low-fat cottage cheese
8 fluid ounces (220ml) skimmed milk
3 eggs
1 tablespoon plain flour
   Dash ground nutmeg
4 ounces (110g) diced fully cooked ham
4 ounces (110g) grated Swiss cheese
2 tablespoons thinly sliced spring onion

351 calories per serving

Prepare pastry shell (see photos 1–6, pages 108–109). Line pastry shell with heavy foil (see photo 7, page 109). Bake in a 450°F (230°C) gas mark 8 oven about 15 minutes or till light brown. Carefully remove foil. Reduce the oven temperature to 325°F (170°C) gas mark 3.

Meanwhile, in a blender container or food processor bowl combine cottage cheese, milk, eggs, flour, and nutmeg. Cover, then blend or process till smooth. Stir in ham, Swiss cheese, and onion. Pour into baked pastry shell. Bake in the 325°F (170°C) gas mark 3 oven for 45 to 50 minutes or till a knife inserted near the centre comes out clean. Let stand for 10 minutes before serving. Makes 6 servings.

Lamb-Aubergine Pie

As the pie bakes, the creamy, cheesy topping puffs up slightly.

Calorie-Trimmed Pastry (see recipe, page 108)
1 pound (450g) minced lamb *or* lean minced beef
4 ounces (110g) chopped onion
12 ounces (350g) peeled, chopped aubergine
8 ounces (225g) tinned stewed tomatoes, cut up
1 ounce (25g) snipped parsley
½ teaspoon salt
¼ teaspoon mustard powder
¼ teaspoon pepper
1 tablespoon cold water
2 teaspoons cornflour
1 slightly beaten egg
8 ounces (225g) low-fat cottage cheese
2 ounces (50g) grated mozzarella cheese

332 calories per serving

Prepare pastry shell (see photos 1–6, pages 108–109). Line pastry shell with heavy foil (see photo 7, page 109). Bake in a 450°F (230°C) gas mark 8 oven about 15 minutes or till light brown. Carefully remove foil. Reduce the oven temperature to 400°F (200°C) gas mark 6.

In a 10-inch (25.5cm) frying pan cook meat and onion till meat is brown. Drain off fat. Stir in aubergine, *undrained* tomatoes, parsley, salt, mustard, and pepper. Bring to boiling and reduce heat. Cover and simmer for 5 to 7 minutes or till aubergine is tender. Stir together water and cornflour, then add to the meat mixture. Cook and stir till thickened and bubbly. Turn into baked pastry shell.

In a small bowl combine egg, cottage cheese, and mozzarella cheese. Spread over meat mixture. Bake in the 400°F (200°C) gas mark 6 oven for 18 to 20 minutes. Cover edges with foil for the last few minutes of baking to prevent overbrowning, if necessary. Let stand for 10 minutes before serving. Makes 6 servings.

Stuffed-Veal Dinner

Company's coming! When dinner guests arrive at the door, diet plans often go out the window. Keep everybody happy with this delightful low-calorie dinner for four. Assemble the entire meal in less than 1½ hours.

Menu

416 calories per serving

- Slimming Stuffed Veal*
- Broccoli Spears
- Mixed Salad*
- Breadsticks
- Strawberries with Strawberry Sauce*

* *see pages 114-117*

Slimming Stuffed Veal

Slimming Stuffed Veal

1 **pound (450g) veal leg round *or* sirloin steak, cut ¼ inch (½cm) thick**
  Salt
  Pepper
2 **slices boiled ham, halved (2 ounces [50g])**
1½ **ounces (40g) sliced mozzarella cheese**
  ½ **teaspoon ground sage**
  3 **tablespoons fine dry bread crumbs**
  2 **tablespoons snipped parsley *or* 2 teaspoons dried parsley flakes**
  ¼ **teaspoon paprika (optional)**
  2 **tablespoons skimmed milk**

220 calories per serving

Trim separable fat from meat (see photo 1, page 24). Cut into four equal pieces (see photo 1). With the smooth side of a meat mallet pound each piece into a rectangle about ⅛ inch (3mm) thick (see photo 2). Sprinkle lightly with salt and pepper. Place *half* of a ham slice and a *quarter* of a cheese slice on each piece of meat. Sprinkle with sage. Fold in sides, then roll up Swiss-roll style (see photo 3). Secure meat rolls with wooden toothpicks.

In a bowl mix bread crumbs, parsley, and paprika, if desired. Dip rolls in milk, then roll in crumb mixture (see photo 4). Place seam side down in a shallow baking dish. Bake in a 350°F (180°C) gas mark 4 oven for 35 to 40 minutes or until done. Makes 4 servings.

1 Using a sharp knife, cut the steak into four equal pieces. By making the pieces as uniform as possible, you can make sure everyone receives the same portion size and number of calories.

2 Using the smooth side of a meat mallet, gently pound each piece of meat into a rectangle, working from the centre to the edges, until the meat is ⅛ inch (3mm) thick.

3 Place the ham and then the cheese on each piece of meat. Sprinkle sage evenly over the ham and cheese. Fold in the sides. This helps prevent the melting cheese from oozing out. Roll up the meat Swiss-roll style. Secure with wooden toothpicks, if necessary.

4 Dip the meat rolls, one at a time, first in the milk (to moisten the surface) and then in the crumb mixture. Roll them around in the mixture to make sure they are well coated. Place the coated meat rolls in a baking dish or tin, seam side down.

Timetable

1¼ hrs. before	● Start preparing the Slimming Stuffed Veal. Place it in the oven 40 minutes before serving time.	
30 mins. before	● Prepare the strawberry sauce and yogurt mixture for the dessert. Place them in the refrigerator to chill. Cut up the strawberries. Cover and chill.	
15 mins. before	● Start cooking the broccoli. While the broccoli cooks, arrange the breadsticks in a basket. ● Prepare the Mixed Salad.	
At Serving Time	● Add the dressing to the salad and toss. Place the salad in salad bowls and sprinkle with cheese. Drain the broccoli and place it in a serving bowl. ● Swirl the strawberry sauce and yogurt mixture together on individual dessert plates. Top it with the strawberries. Chill until dessert time.	

Strawberries with Strawberry Sauce

12 ounces (350g) fresh *or* frozen
    unsweetened strawberries
2   tablespoons honey
2   tablespoons brandy *or* rum
2   ounces (50g) natural low-fat yogurt
1   tablespoon sifted icing sugar

104 calories per serving

If using fresh strawberries, wash berries and drain, then remove hulls. Thaw strawberries, if frozen. Reserve 16 strawberries. In a food processor bowl or blender container combine remaining strawberries, honey, and brandy. Cover and process or blend till smooth. Transfer to a bowl. Cover and chill. In a small bowl mix yogurt and sugar. Cover and chill. Slice reserved berries, reserving four whole berries for garnish.

To serve, spoon strawberry sauce onto shallow dessert plates. Swirl some of the yogurt mixture through sauce. Arrange sliced berries atop. Garnish with whole strawberries. Serves 4.

Mixed Salad

See photo, page 112.

1¾ ounces (45g) torn lettuce leaves
1   tomato, cut into wedges
2   ounces (50g) sliced radishes
½   small cucumber *or* courgette
2   ounces (50g) reduced-oil salad
    dressing
2   tablespoons grated Parmesan cheese

38 calories per serving

In a bowl combine torn lettuce leaves, tomato, and radishes. Run a fork lengthwise down cucumber or courgette to score it. Cut into ⅛-inch (3mm) slices, then add to salad. Add salad dressing; toss gently to coat. Spoon salad onto dishes. Sprinkle with cheese. Makes 4 servings.

Tomatoes Vinaigrette

A quick-to-fix alternative to Mixed Salad.

4   tomatoes
1½   ounces (40g) sliced fresh mushrooms
1   tablespoon sliced spring onion
3   fluid ounces (80ml) reduced-oil
     salad dressing
     Lettuce

40 calories per serving

Peel tomatoes, if desired. Cut into wedges. Place tomatoes, mushrooms, and onion into a bowl. Pour dressing over vegetables. Cover and chill about 4 hours. Stir once or twice. Before serving, line individual salad plates with lettuce. Remove vegetables from dressing with a slotted spoon and arrange on lettuce. Drizzle with dressing. Makes 4 servings.

Orange Fluff

A great dessert option you can make in advance.

½   teaspoon finely grated orange peel
8   fluid ounces (220ml) orange juice
2   teaspoons unflavoured gelatin
⅛   teaspoon ground nutmeg
1   egg white
2   ounces (50g) frozen whipped topping,
    thawed

85 calories per serving

In a small saucepan combine orange peel, orange juice, gelatin, and nutmeg. Let stand for 5 minutes. Heat and stir till gelatin dissolves. Remove from the heat. Chill mixture till partially set. In a small mixer bowl beat egg white with an electric mixer till foamy. Gradually add gelatin mixture, beating at high speed till fluffy, 1 to 2 minutes. Fold in topping. (Chill till mixture mounds, if necessary.) Spoon into four dessert dishes. Chill until set. Makes 4 servings.

6 ounces (175g)
strawberries with
2 fluid ounces (110ml)
light cream
and 1 teaspoon
icing sugar
146 calories

Lettuce wedge with 1
tablespoon French
salad dressing
92 calories

3 ounces (75g) cooked
French beans with
1 tablespoon butter
132 calories

1 medium baked potato
with 1 tablespoon
soured cream and 1
rasher cooked streaky
bacon, crumbled
214 calories

Fried chicken breast half
with skin (4 ounces
[110g])
234 calories

818 calories

Calorie Countdown

Every dieter longs to unlock the secret of successful dieting: cutting calories, but not losing fresh flavours and taste. Impossible, you say? Just look at the example above and you'll see how easy it is to cleverly trim calories. Look even closer and you'll see that what you reduce is calories, not the good taste of the food you enjoy.

Why lose weight?

Aside from the desire for an improved personal appearance, why should you take a look at shedding extra pounds? Excess body fat puts unnecessary strain on the joints, vital organs, and respiratory and circulatory systems. Obese people also tend to have a higher incidence of high blood pressure and diabetes.

The big C—calories

So, what are calories? Calories are much more than just a number attached to a portion of food. Calories are units that measure the amount of energy your body receives from the food you eat. Here's how they work.

For every 3,500 calories you consume, your body stores one pound of fat, or energy. When you use fewer calories than your body takes in, you gain weight. And when you use more calories than you consume, you lose weight.

6 ounces (175g)
strawberries with
2 fluid ounces (110ml)
skimmed milk
77 calories

Lettuce wedge with
1 tablespoon oil-free
French salad dressing
39 calories

3 ounces (75g) cooked
French beans
30 calories

1 medium baked potato
with 1 tablespoon
natural yogurt
and snipped chives
152 calories

Roasted or baked
chicken breast half
without skin
(4 ounces [110g])
206 calories

504 calories

Enough is enough!

Well, how can you tell when you've had enough calories? To determine your calorie needs, first calculate how many calories your body needs each day to maintain its current weight (convert your weight to pounds—one stone is 14 pounds—and multiply by 15). Then determine how many calories you need to eliminate from your diet each day in order to lose weight (subtract either 500 or 1,000 calories from the number needed to maintain your present weight). By subtracting 500 calories, you can expect to lose about 1 pound a week, and by subtracting 1,000 calories, you can expect to lose about 2 pounds a week. It's hard to get the more than 40 nutrients your body needs daily by consuming less than 1,000 calories per day. So when dieting, try to keep your daily intake above 1,000 calories.

Keeping it off

No matter how much weight you lose, the real challenge is keeping it off. By making reasonable changes in your life-style, you can make your new-found weight loss a permanent one. Be sure to include some type of physical activity as a part of your daily routine.

Exercising

Exercise not only burns calories, but improves fitness and mental relaxation as well. Plan to get regular exercise rather than occasional strenuous activity. The best way to have a regular exercise program and stick with it is to tailor it to your individual life-style and needs. Even chores like mowing the lawn, spading the garden, or shovelling snow offer exercise.

Before starting an exercise routine, make sure you are ready medically. When your doctor has given you the OK, plan to make exercise part of your daily routine. Whether you decide to jog, swim, or cycle, set a pace that's comfortable for you. Start any exercise off slowly. Exercise long enough to get a good workout, but not so long that you feel fatigued. Then, slowly increase the time you spend exercising. The reward of a healthier, leaner body will be worth the effort.

**Milk-Cheese
Group**

**Bread-Cereal
Group**

Slimming Success

Variety is the spice of life! So why not make it the spice of your diet as well? The Five Basic Food Groups allow you to make choices in your food selection without time-consuming calculations. Choose the proper number of servings from each category, and you'll be sure to receive all the nutrients you need each day.

Variety, the spice of diet!

Even when you're counting calories, it's easy to make meals extra special. Learning how to combine different types of food can add a world of variety to your meals. Planning your meals around the Five Basic Food Groups allows you plenty of flexibility. The five food groups are: Milk-Cheese; Bread-Cereal; Vegetable-Fruit; Meat, Poultry, Fish, Nuts, and Beans; and Fats, Sweets, and Alcohol. When choosing foods from each category, keep these calorie-conscious tips in mind.

Milk-Cheese Group

The foods in this group contain calcium, riboflavin, protein, and vitamins A, B_6, and B_{12}. Choose dairy products made with skimmed or low-fat milk.

Recommended daily servings: 3 servings for children 9 to 12, 4 for teens, 2 for adults, 3 for pregnant women, and 4 for nursing mothers.

A serving is 8 fluid ounces (220ml) of skimmed milk, 8 ounces (225g) of low-fat yogurt, 16 ounces (450g) of cottage cheese, 2 ounces (50g) cup of Parmesan cheese, or 12 ounces (350g) of ice milk.

**Vegetable-Fruit
Group**

**Meat, Poultry,
Fish, Nuts, and
Beans Group**

Bread-Cereal Group

This group of foods includes breads, pasta, and a selection of whole grain products. Look for whole grain or enriched breads and pastas. Many breakfast cereals are fortified with needed nutrients.

Recommended daily servings: Plan four servings from this group each day.

A serving is 1 slice of whole grain bread, 3½ ounces of cooked cereal, macaroni, noodles, or rice, or 1 ounce of ready-to-eat cereal.

Vegetable-Fruit Group

Fruits and vegetables provide vitamins A and C and fibre. With the exception of avocados and olives, all fruits and vegetables are naturally low in calories. Choose unsweetened fruits—fresh, frozen, canned, or dried. Fresh fruits are best because they are more filling than other options.

Recommended daily servings: Plan four servings daily.

A serving is 3 ounces of any fruit or vegetable or 1 medium orange, apple, or baked potato, or a lettuce wedge.

Meat, Poultry, Fish, Nuts, and Beans Group

Control calories by remembering that your body needs only 6 ounces of meat a day. Fish and poultry are best for calorie counters because they have less fat. Lean meats cooked without added fat also work well. Occasionally include dried beans and peas for variety.

Recommended daily servings: Plan two servings daily, but be sure to vary the source.

A serving is 2 to 3 ounces of lean, cooked meat, 2 eggs, 3 ounces of cooked dried beans, peas, or soybeans, 2 tablespoons of peanut butter, or 1½ to 3½ ounces of nuts, sesame seeds, or sunflower seeds.

Fats, Sweets, and Alcohol Group

Mayonnaise, candy, sugar, soft drinks, and alcoholic beverages fall into this category. Because they are high in calories—but low in minerals, vitamins, and protein—they provide little or no nutritional value. Try to minimize foods in this category. Use of these foods in your diet depends on the number of calories you can afford to consume.

Nutrition Analysis Chart

Use these analyses to compare nutritional values of different recipes. This information was calculated using Agriculture Handbook Number 456, published by the United States Department of Agriculture, as the primary source. Figures are based on the ingredients used in the American version of each recipe.

In compiling the nutrition analyses, we made the following assumptions:
- For all of the main-dish meat recipes, the nutrition analyses were calculated using weights or measures for cooked lean meat.

- Garnishes and optional ingredients were not included in the nutrition analyses.
- If a marinade was brushed over the food during cooking, the analysis includes all of the marinade.
- When two ingredient options appear in a recipe, calculations were made using the first one.
- For ingredients of variable weight (such as "2½- to 3-pound [1kg125g to 1kg350g] chicken") or for recipes with a serving range ("4 to 6 servings"), calculations were made using the first figure.

	Per Serving						U.S. Recommended Daily Allowances Per Serving (%)							
	Calories	Protein (g)	Carbohydrate (g)	Fat (g)	Sodium (mg)	Potassium (mg)	Protein	Vitamin A	Vitamin C	Thiamine	Riboflavin	Niacin	Calcium	Iron
Main Dishes, Beef														
Beef Eater's Bounty (p. 20)	203	17	10	11	315	525	27	37	35	9	23	17	14	17
Beef Stroganoff Cups (p. 105)	220	16	11	12	125	310	25	5	3	9	18	19	7	11
Beefy Borscht (p. 38)	150	17	9	5	667	461	26	27	52	5	11	14	5	15
Beefy Vegetable-Sauced Pasta (p. 57)	305	24	32	9	663	804	37	41	127	22	19	33	5	29
Burgundy Beef (p. 26)	176	22	7	4	68	393	33	61	7	5	11	21	3	16
Cheese-Stuffed Burgers (p. 51)	245	28	4	13	251	351	42	10	11	8	17	27	8	20
Joint of Roast Beef with Mushroom Sauce (p. 75)	163	25	2	5	308	302	39	0	5	13	25	1	17	0
Lemon-Marinated Steak (p. 81)	158	21	1	7	127	248	32	1	10	4	9	20	1	14
Orange-Beef Stir-Fry (p. 92)	183	21	19	4	710	717	32	62	257	16	24	22	15	20
Pepper Steak (p. 60)	229	21	25	5	826	417	32	10	99	14	15	22	3	19
Quick Beef Stew (p. 62)	249	25	25	6	919	568	38	20	36	10	16	29	4	20
Roast Round of Beef with Vegetables (p. 74)	169	19	10	6	81	345	30	9	19	6	12	18	4	17
Saucy Steaks (p. 27)	300	22	29	10	570	256	35	9	4	11	15	21	10	15
Sesame Veal (p. 93)	289	25	8	17	178	562	38	27	58	14	21	30	4	19
Sherry-Marinated Steaks (p. 78)	164	21	4	4	84	287	33	4	6	4	12	22	2	16
Slimming Stuffed Veal (p. 114)	220	23	5	11	383	261	36	4	5	9	15	20	11	15
South Seas Steak Pinwheels (p. 51)	160	17	16	3	42	507	26	28	114	6	11	18	3	15
Spicy Beef Stew (p. 24)	160	18	15	4	526	673	28	172	109	11	16	20	8	17
Taco-Filled Courgette Shells (p. 33)	191	20	6	10	198	465	30	15	46	8	16	23	11	16
Tangy Beef and Swiss Sandwiches (Whole Wheat Bread) (p. 12)	258	20	18	12	507	353	31	19	32	10	17	13	34	16
(Pitta Bread) (p. 12)	230	19	12	11	356	280	30	19	32	8	16	10	32	13
(Tortillas) (p. 12)	285	20	22	13	356	280	31	19	32	5	20	14	36	17
Terrific Taco Pie (p. 108)	367	20	24	21	666	279	31	19	27	16	18	24	9	16

	Per Serving						U.S. Recommended Daily Allowances Per Serving (%)							
	Calories	Protein (g)	Carbohydrate (g)	Fat (g)	Sodium (mg)	Potassium (mg)	Protein	Vitamin A	Vitamin C	Thiamine	Riboflavin	Niacin	Calcium	Iron

Main Dishes, Beef (continued)

	Calories	Protein (g)	Carbohydrate (g)	Fat (g)	Sodium (mg)	Potassium (mg)	Protein	Vitamin A	Vitamin C	Thiamine	Riboflavin	Niacin	Calcium	Iron
Veal à l'Orange (p. 75)	183	20	5	8	62	286	31	5	25	6	12	21	1	14
Veal Stew (p. 26)	221	19	20	8	314	847	29	146	89	13	17	27	7	21

Main Dishes, Eggs and Cheese

	Calories	Protein (g)	Carbohydrate (g)	Fat (g)	Sodium (mg)	Potassium (mg)	Protein	Vitamin A	Vitamin C	Thiamine	Riboflavin	Niacin	Calcium	Iron
Asparagus-Cheese Omelettes (p. 96)	235	18	8	15	474	456	28	36	36	18	35	9	14	19
Cheese and Fruit Salad (p. 20)	285	14	27	15	451	283	21	20	12	5	17	2	41	7
Cheese and Veggie Sandwiches (Whole Wheat Bread) (p. 14)	188	16	22	5	523	376	24	47	45	10	15	7	12	10
(Tortillas) (p. 14)	215	16	25	6	373	303	24	47	44	5	18	8	14	11
Chicken and Artichoke Omelettes (p. 98)	248	24	10	13	496	492	38	21	9	11	30	19	14	15
Egg Salad Surprise (Rye Bread) (p. 14)	293	17	20	17	511	539	27	39	53	14	22	7	21	19
(Pitta Bread) (p. 14)	265	16	13	16	361	466	25	39	53	11	21	4	20	16
Eggs Olé (p. 42)	286	21	29	10	605	428	33	42	73	12	21	28	9	21
Greek Omelettes (p. 99)	241	18	5	17	461	410	27	136	35	12	26	2	22	22
Pizza Omelettes (p. 99)	256	6	18	10	658	378	25	40	35	12	20	7	13	15
Poached Eggs with Prawn Sauce (p. 45)	194	19	7	10	361	419	29	128	35	9	21	5	23	21
Southwestern Omelettes (p. 98)	259	17	9	17	468	320	27	49	96	11	24	5	18	18
Vegetable Carbonara (p. 54)	245	16	27	9	243	344	24	57	26	11	18	10	22	16
Vegetable-Tofu Soup (p. 39)	261	17	24	12	1110	423	25	79	17	12	21	7	39	15

Main Dishes, Fish and Seafood

	Calories	Protein (g)	Carbohydrate (g)	Fat (g)	Sodium (mg)	Potassium (mg)	Protein	Vitamin A	Vitamin C	Thiamine	Riboflavin	Niacin	Calcium	Iron
Crab with Lime Sauce (p. 87)	195	26	2	9	477	280	40	70	9	16	7	21	7	7
Fancy Fish Fillets (p. 80)	147	21	10	2	160	708	33	7	89	10	12	12	14	9
Fettuccine with Clam Sauce (p. 56)	238	15	33	5	625	367	23	64	16	20	22	14	24	24
Orange-Ginger Lobster (p. 50)	150	21	4	5	274	268	33	4	26	9	5	9	8	5
Pineapple-Sauced Fish (p. 81)	112	21	6	0	204	412	32	3	11	4	5	17	4	6
Poached Fish with Lemon-Dill Sauce (p. 45)	253	23	4	13	70	411	35	55	3	12	10	18	5	3
Poached Halibut in Tangy Lime Sauce (p. 44)	180	24	4	7	270	534	37	13	7	5	7	39	5	4
Prawn and Spinach Stir-Fry (p. 93)	174	15	13	8	131	675	23	109	88	9	10	15	11	18
Salmon-Rice Bake (p. 8)	307	26	21	13	707	453	40	13	17	17	22	38	36	13
Scallops Italian (p. 56)	257	25	35		781	634	39	27	30	27	15	22	12	23
Seaside Sandwiches (Tortillas) (p. 15)	232	14	23	9	270	265	22	42	20	9	14	12	11	14
(Whole Wheat Bread) (p. 15)	205	14	19	8	420	337	22	42	20	14	11	11	9	13
Shellfish Soup (p. 38)	176	20	22	1	802	554	30	95	16	7	17	10	28	12
Spicy Steamed Fish (p. 84)	197	49	9	20	154	703	38	23	36	9	6	49	3	8
Stacked Prawn Creole (p. 104)	216	23	27	2	599	675	35	28	84	15	16	23	14	17
Steamed Salmon with Horseradish Sauce (p. 86)	208	24	6	9	235	448	37	53	3	12	15	17	11	3
Steamed Snapper and Squash (p. 86)	251	25	21	7	480	472	38	14	36	21	6	6	4	10
Tempting Tuna Salad (p. 20)	213	22	8	10	436	349	34	40	63	7	18	33	21	12
Tropical Salmon Salad (p. 21)	237	25	13	9	591	568	39	6	29	8	17	47	27	9
Vegetable-Sauced Fish Fillets (p. 87)	201	29	7	5	424	570	44	44	5	8	13	15	12	6

Main Dishes, Lamb

	Calories	Protein (g)	Carbohydrate (g)	Fat (g)	Sodium (mg)	Potassium (mg)	Protein	Vitamin A	Vitamin C	Thiamine	Riboflavin	Niacin	Calcium	Iron
Greek-Style Stuffed Tomatoes (p. 32)	196	16	22	6	54	634	24	29	60	14	16	19	7	14
Lamb-Aubergine Pie (p. 111)	333	27	26	13	615	494	41	15	26	19	25	23	14	15
Lamb Chops and Vegetables (p. 27)	148	19	7	5	360	442	29	13	69	10	13	22	3	10
Lamb Chops with Lemon-Mustard Sauce (p. 48)	142	21	2	5	207	252	32	0	3	8	12	22	2	10

	Per Serving						U.S. Recommended Daily Allowances Per Serving (%)								
	Calories	Protein (g)	Carbohydrate (g)	Fat (g)	Sodium (mg)	Potassium (mg)	Protein	Vitamin A	Vitamin C	Thiamine	Riboflavin	Niacin	Calcium	Iron
Main Dishes, Pork (continued)														
Oriental Soup (p. 36)	171	21	7	7	1172	351	32	8	18	38	17	24	2	18
Pineapple-Ham Kababs (p. 50)	204	22	12	8	774	339	34	2	46	37	13	20	2	17
Pork and Courgette Stir-Fry (p. 92)	234	20	10	13	784	547	31	83	24	49	21	28	5	19
Pork-and-Spinach-Filled Vegetables (p. 30)	294	17	18	18	407	597	25	91	198	29	19	18	11	20
Pork Pot Pie (p. 110)	321	20	29	14	499	388	31	93	20	35	21	21	9	17
Pork Strips in Pineapple Sauce (p. 63)	245	18	24	9	116	519	28	89	31	35	16	20	6	18
Pork with Curry Relish (p. 74)	175	18	5	9	110	243	28	5	2	45	12	21	1	14
Roast Pork Florentine (p. 72)	270	29	8	13	390	514	44	80	21	70	21	32	6	26
Sweet-Sour Pork Pancakes (p. 104)	267	18	32	8	306	374	28	33	43	27	17	16	8	14
White Lasagne (p. 57)	284	26	26	8	623	434	41	29	59	30	30	16	30	12
Main Dishes, Poultry														
Brandied Tarragon Chicken (p. 69)	217	28	1	3	134	1	43	2	0	5	16	55	2	10
Carrot-Stuffed Chicken Rolls (p. 66)	214	29	10	5	185	359	45	164	14	8	15	56	6	13
Chicken-Barley Soup (p. 38)	126	16	10	3	713	303	24	56	6	4	7	23	3	7
Chicken-Chilli Pepper Quiche (p. 110)	334	22	25	16	522	378	33	20	30	14	27	18	33	11
Chicken Parmesan (p. 68)	206	32	4	7	89	138	49	45	18	7	20	54	13	13
Curried Pinwheels (p. 69)	225	29	15	6	72	130	45	3	3	6	14	56	3	12
Curried Turkeywiches (Pitta Bread) (p. 15)	261	22	22	8	134	311	34	8	29	9	11	23	5	10
(Tortillas) (p. 15)	276	21	24	10	134	311	33	8	29	4	14	26	7	13
Fruity Chicken Salad (p. 18)	184	22	14	5	287	698	33	89	98	10	18	30	12	17
Garlic Chicken (p. 90)	300	35	18	9	904	342	54	123	31	22	21	65	6	22
Ham-Filled Chicken Rolls (p. 68)	267	37	4	11	499	153	57	9	6	21	21	59	4	18
Hawaiian Chicken (p. 44)	191	29	10	3	660	134	44	3	24	9	15	54	3	13
Hot Turkey Salad (p. 62)	154	19	9	5	337	373	30	75	70	8	17	29	8	17
Sausage and Cabbage Soup (p. 39)	215	13	14	0	526	406	4	3	79	6	4	5	4	3
Summer Fruit-Chicken Salad (p. 21)	241	20	27	6	185	651	32	29	26	7	15	31	6	11
Turkey Pancakes (p. 105)	280	30	27	6	422	582	46	8	12	13	27	32	18	12
Turkey-Stuffed Tomato Shells (p. 33)	219	22	14	9	422	767	33	42	86	10	18	30	11	14
Turkey-Vegetable Casserole (p. 9)	247	13	30	9	431	171	7	51	7	6	4	8	3	8
Zesty Chicken (p. 44)	172	29	6	3	123	174	44	11	31	7	14	56	3	11
Miscellaneous														
Calorie-Counter's Pancakes (p. 102)	118	2	6	1	17	42	3	1	0	4	5	2	3	2
Calorie-Trimmed Pastry (p. 108)	143	4	16	7	140	32	6	0	9	6	6	1	4	4
Mixed Salad (p. 117)	38	2	4	2	202	213	4	10	25	3	4	2	6	4
Orange Fluff (p. 117)	85	3	10	4	14	136	4	3	52	4	2	1	1	1
Salad Dressing Base (p. 18)	16	1	2	1	74	22	1	2	0	1	2	0	2	1
Strawberries with Strawberry Sauce (p. 117)	104	1	21	1	9	209	2	2	110	3	6	4	4	7
Tomatoes Vinaigrette (p. 117)	40	2	7	1	161	343	3	23	48	6	5	6	2	4